SKETCHING ON LOCATION

MATTHEW BREHM

Kendall Hunt
publishing company

Kendall Hunt
publishing company

www.kendallhunt.com
Send all inquiries to:
4050 Westmark Drive
Dubuque, IA 52004-1840

Copyright © 2012 by Matthew Brehm

ISBN 978-1-4652-0526-1

Printed in the United States of America
10 9 8 7 6 5 4 3 2

This book is dedicated to:

My students and fellow sketchers—past, present, and future.
My own love of sketching is inspired and amplified by your work
and dedication to the craft.

My brother, Greg, who first introduced me to the study of architecture,
the skill of drawing, and the glories of Rome.

My parents, for your love and support over many years,
and for setting high expectations while always keeping me grounded.

My sons, Will and Sam. Your sense of wonder and
your sense of humor have sustained me more than you know.

And most of all to my wife, Patty. Every day, your love, support,
and friendship help me become who I strive to be.

Contents

ACKNOWLEDGMENTS

Many thanks are due to individuals and organizations who have helped along the way as I developed the drawing, writing and teaching skills that ultimately contributed to this book. They are too numerous to name, but among them are several who deserve special recognition and my most sincere appreciation:

Kendall Hunt Publishing Company—especially Kimberly Elliott for her energy and help in conceiving the book, and Beth Trowbridge for her practical assistance in bringing it to press.

The University of Idaho for its support as I developed the approaches to teaching contained here, and also for providing the time necessary for the writing of this book.

My colleagues at the University of Oregon and the University of Idaho, for their mentorship and collegiality.

Daniel Herbert, whose assistance with the writing of my graduate thesis was invaluable. I learned more about the craft of writing from Dan than from all my other teachers combined.

Richard Piccolo, who gave me my first real education in sketching from observation, my first and most memorable lessons in watercolor, and who has been an essential resource in the development of the annual study program I conduct in Rome.

Gabriel Campanario, founder of Urban Sketchers, who has worked tirelessly to elevate the value of sketching on location and to connect sketchers around the world.

Román Montoto, who for many years has been a great friend and cherished colleague.

MTB
Rome, Italy
June, 2012

CHAPTER

1

INTRODUCTION

"Sketching on Location" means making a relatively brief and direct drawing of a subject within view of the artist. It means making a complete sketch on-site, rather than working from photographs or memory. Sketching on location can be done anywhere, and the subject could be a building or a public square, a piece of furniture or a person, a mountain range or a solitary tree, or any collection of these and many other elements. Regardless of the subject matter, the most essential component of sketching on location is direct observation. Carefully

Figure 1.1 Piazza Navona
Rome, IT
June 1, 2007
Graphite, Acrylic Ink (Sepia), Watercolor, on Aquabee Plate Bristol (12" × 9")
45 minutes

observing our surroundings and making sketches of what we observe is one the most effective ways we can learn about and understand the physical world around us. Sketching is a way of recording this observation, and it also serves to intensify and extend the act observing. Sketching on location has been practiced for hundreds, if not thousands, of years, and it is enjoying renewed interest around the world as people who sketch make connections and share their work through online venues. Sketching on location is a very fruitful and enjoyable activity, and it brings a wonderful sense of accomplishment and satisfaction as one develops the skill over time. As with any skill, and particularly those that involve working with the hands, sketching is best viewed as a craft, because it requires a thorough knowledge of materials and techniques and a specialized form of manual dexterity that puts knowledge into practice. Although it is a specialized skill, sketching may truly be learned by anyone who has the motivation to practice and develop their ability over time.

In addition to doing it for simple enjoyment, sketching is a purposeful activity. This is one of the distinctions between "sketching" and "doodling." Both involve making marks on paper, but "doodling" connotes a relatively aimless activity that is intended only to occupy one's time, with little other purpose. Sketching from

Figure 1.2 The Garden Lounge
Moscow, ID
January 23, 2009
Copic Multiliner (Cobalt) in a Moleskine Pocket Sketchbook (7" × 5.5")
15 minutes

observation, even if it is idle sketching that helps the passing of time, has, at the very least, the purpose of learning about what is being drawn or building skills for drawing. Sketching from the imagination, to generate ideas or solve graphic problems, also has a purpose, and is therefore in a different category than doodling. Sketching from observation is useful for anyone, but environmental designers (architects, landscape architects, interior designers, virtual reality designers, etc.), especially, have much to gain from the practice. The ability to capture an existing spatial environment through sketching leads directly to an improved ability to quickly convey an accurate depiction of a proposed environment. Students of design have perhaps the most to gain from developing the practice and making it a fundamental aspect of their working lives, but sketching is readily available to anyone with a curiosity about the world around them and the motivation to develop their abilities.

The focus of this book is on recording observations of existing places, whether they are grand and historic (Figure I.I) or humble and quotidian (Figure I.2). The techniques and principles can be applied to a wide variety of subjects. This introduction provides background on the subject of sketching on location, including a brief overview of its history and some suggested attitudes toward learning and developing the skill.

Brief History of Sketching on Location

Drawing has been a human activity since the dawn of recorded history, though the way we currently use the term "sketching" is relatively recent. Originally, the word appears to have come from the Greek *skhédios*, which means "done extemporaneously" or without preparation. The Italian *schizzare* (literally "to splash") came from the Latin *schedius*, meaning "hastily made." The word and its meaning—a "rough drawing intended to serve as the model for a finished painting"—emerged in the Dutch word *schets* during the 17th century. It has a roughly parallel meaning in literature to describe a brief, unfinished, rough draft of a story. More recently, the act of sketching has become recognized for its own sake. Today, in other words, a sketch need not lead to anything else, but can be considered a finished work on its own.

Regardless of how long we've been using some version of the word "sketch," people have been making quick, informal graphic images to tell stories or simply to show what they've observed since prehistoric times. The oldest recorded cave paintings date to over 30,000 years ago, and these are only what have survived by virtue of their protection from the elements (for comparison, the earliest written languages that we know of date to approximately 3000 BCE). The skill displayed in these images strongly suggests that drawing was a common means of communication, and that it was actually practiced as an elevated craft even at this early date. However, there was a general lack of available materials appropriate for sketching as we know it today. Papyrus and parchment were used from ancient times through the Middle Ages for writing, drawing, and illuminating manuscripts, but these supports were generally too precious to be used for sketching and too expensive to be available to common artists. Laid paper became available and reasonably affordable in the late 14th century, and with it came a dramatic increase in the making of preparatory sketches (also known as *cartoons*) that painters and fresco artists would create in the process of designing more formal artwork. There are many "Old Master Drawings" from this period onward that show painters using drawing on paper primarily as a means of study and practice, particularly regarding human form and anatomy, and also for developing compositional strategies prior to painting. The most common media for these drawings include chalk, charcoal, pen and ink, and light washes of various pigments. The wood-encased graphite pencil first became available in the 17th century, approximately 100 years after the discovery of an enormous deposit of very pure graphite in Cumbria, England. Wove paper, which is smoother than laid paper and more able to receive fine lines and dry media, became more readily available in the late 18th century, further increasing access to sketching materials for the common artist.

Figure 1.3 Rio Terrà dei Catecumeni
Venice, IT
July 31, 2009
B Pencil on Fabriano Ruvido paper (9" × 12")
40 minutes

Figure I.4   Santa Maria in Trastevere
Rome, IT
July 18, 2010
B Pencil and Watercolor in Moleskine Large Watercolor Sketchbook (5" × 8")
30 minutes

Sketching developed further as a form of study during the time of the "Grand Tour" in continental Europe. This was a type of educational travel, beginning in the 17th and continuing through the 19th centuries, coming to an end as the rail system allowed easier movement throughout the continent. The tour was primarily for well-to-do young Englishmen, and more rarely, for women. "Grand tourists" would be guided by an experienced traveler, who, having been paid by the young voyager's family, would lead him to the major and minor sights of classical antiquity, primarily in Italy. For the majority of grand tourists, the trip was akin to present-day visits to foreign locations, during which the tourist is most often a passive observer rather than a more engaged traveler. For some grand tourists, however, especially those anticipating a career in architecture or an allied field, place-recording through sketching and measured drawings was a significant component of the tour. During roughly the same period of time as the Grand Tour, but extending into the 20th century, the Ecole des Beaux Arts awarded the winners of its "Grand Prix de Rome" competition with a period of study in Rome—usually from three to five years. Early versions of the competition were focused on painting and sculpture, with an architecture category being added in 1722. Winners and runners-up would be housed together in Rome, creating a sort of academy in miniature, and their primary assignment was to document the multitude of classical antiquities in and around Rome in their own sketches, drawings, paintings, and sculpture. In the mid- to late 19th century in the United States, organizations began to appear that fostered sketching skills among young architects. The Philadelphia Sketch Club was founded in 1860 to provide affordable drawing classes and to create a venue for artists to exhibit their work. While not exclusively focused on sketching, it is notable that the group's name prominently

Figure 1.5   Pavello de Mies Van der Rohe
Barcelona, SP
July 4, 2009
Copic Multiliner SP (Olive) in Moleskine Large Watercolor Sketchbook (5" × 8")
20 minutes

includes the word "sketch." Similarly, the Chicago Sketching Club (subsequently The Chicago Architectural Club, founded in 1885), was created as a quasi-professional, quasi-social organization that included "sketching evenings" where members would compete for prizes. These clubs in Philadelphia and Chicago were among the first of their kind, but there soon followed similar clubs in other cities, creating new social networks with sketching on location being one of the primary means to develop skills and camaraderie among peers.

These clubs, unfortunately, did not last long. They were part of an age (related to the Beaux Arts, Arts and Crafts, and Naturalist Painting movements), that was to be replaced by a variety of "modern" movements in the arts. These newer movements valued abstraction over representation, the clean, rational lines of a machine over the quaint street scenes of a medieval village, or large blocks and sprays of color over visually identifiable humans or places. While the new approaches unquestionably expanded the boundaries of artistic expression, they brought with them a tendency to dismiss representational art as being inconsequential, and their rise was inevitably matched by the fall of observational sketching as a rigorous study in all but the most traditional of academies. It is true that the initial waves of modernists had been trained in the traditional manner through observational drawing, and that this training helped position them to make their breakthroughs, but eventually the importance of observational drawing was dramatically diminished. A similar change occurred in the design fields, especially in architecture, as visual representations of proposed projects gave way to abstracted diagrams and an emphasis on orthographic drawings.

Despite these changes in attitude toward representational art, some institutions carried on the tradition of location sketching as a means of absorbing places and cultures, and as a way of studying architecture and urban spaces, particularly in "Old World" settings. Study-abroad tours have become an integral aspect of a university education since at least the 1960s, especially in architecture programs. Varying in duration from a few weeks to as much as an academic year, the programs are often built around semi-formal courses, where structured classroom learning is merely an adjunct, at most, to the direct experience of visiting important sites and recording them via hand-drawing in a sketchbook—a modern derivation of the Grand Tour. The sketchbook extends the traveler's abilities for place-recording far beyond the capabilities of a camera. The time spent at a particular location is necessarily increased, and personal observations and/or historic information can be associated with the sketches.

While study-abroad programs were continuing (and increasing in popularity), there were other factors that led to a general decrease in the recognized importance of sketching on location. With the advent of widespread personal computing in the 1990s, digital photography became the most common means of capturing images on location, and digital design and drawing tools became the de facto methods for graphic communication in design schools. With the exception of study-abroad experiences, where hand-sketching was still somewhat of a priority, the expectation diminished for students to sketch from observation. The newer generation of teachers was populated with former students who had not been trained to draw by hand, and the emphasis on sketching continued to fade. In the first years of the new millennium, sketching by hand had become a rarity in design schools. Nonetheless, the practice was being carried on by a small cadre of design students and practitioners, as well as people outside the design disciplines, if only as a hobby.

While the emphasis on digital graphics overshadowed the tradition of drawing by hand, the communicative power of the Internet led to sketchers discovering one another and making personal connections around the world. Thanks to these connections, the practice of sketching appears to be gaining in popularity. This apparent resurgence might simply be a factor of increased worldwide communication—it might seem as though there are more people sketching because they are increasingly making their presence known through online forums. Or it could be an actual revival of the practice on a grand scale, in direct response (or reaction) to the onslaught of digital media over the past 20 years. My sense is that the latter is more likely—that, as the result of so many sketchers sharing their work online, more people every day are becoming exposed to and interested in the

Figure 1.6 Ira Keller Fountain
Portland, OR
October 2, 2010
Watercolor in Hand-Book Journal (10" × 8")
45 minutes

practice. Perhaps people have always sketched on location, whether or not they have been associated with the Grand Tour, or the professions of architecture and allied fields, or a university study-abroad program. The major difference is that now these people have numerous venues for sharing their work, almost in real time, with others who have a similar passion for location drawing. And these connections are not only on a local level—they are truly global in scope. The connectivity provided by the Internet is not an especially new phenomenon, of course, but its extensive use by analog sketch artists is fairly recent, with the most significant growth to date occurring since about 2007 or 2008.

Another distinguishing factor in this trend relates to demographics. Where the Grand Tour, professionally oriented sketch clubs, and typical study-abroad programs have all been defined to some degree by exclusivity—that is, exclusive of those who hadn't or haven't the wherewithal to participate—the Internet has created social networks based around location sketching that are open to all. The only costs of admission are a willingness to share one's sketches and ready access to the Internet. While the latter is admittedly not yet universal, particularly

Figure I.7   View from the Palatine Hill
Rome, IT
July 9, 2011
2B Pencil on on Canson Classic Cream Drawing paper (9" × 12")
40 minutes

outside of industrialized nations, things do appear to be heading in that direction. So a form of democratization is occurring, where location drawing is no longer the province of the well-to-do. The democratization provided by the Internet has created a significant change in focus—while many of the sketchers who share their work online are architects by training, or illustrators, landscape architects, animators, etc., a growing number could be considered lay people who lack formal training in the craft of sketching or graphic communication.

Figure 1.8   Sister's Brew Coffeehouse
Moscow, ID
January 17, 2010
Uniball Vision Micro Black and Watercolor in Moleskine Large Watercolor Sketchbook (5" × 8")
40 minutes

As well, the subject matter for location drawing is no longer limited to specific geographies—it is no longer only the "important" places that rank as sketch-worthy. On the contrary, a vast number of the sketches being shared online are of the artists' hometowns and their vicinity. Travel sketches remain a common, and often highly valued, subject for work shared online, but sketches of an artist's home turf are becoming even more common. Because sketch artists live all over the world, viewing their work online provides an opportunity to travel vicariously through their drawings. There are many online sources used by location sketchers to share their work and form connections. Individuals often have a weblog where they can periodically display and comment on their own work, and where visitors can engage in discussion with the artist. Group blogs bring individuals together, usually around a common theme—sketching in nature, or urban sketching, for example. Photo-sharing websites have been co-opted by sketchers to display their work in the form of an online catalog. Examples of these resources are listed at the end of this book.

Some sketch artists have begun to use digital tools such as tablets and "paint" programs for mobile devices, but the overwhelming majority of artists sharing their work online use analog media and post scans or photos of their physical sketchbooks. Portable tablets and touch-screen phones allow for digital sketching on the go, but since the most critical aspect of sketching is observation, it doesn't matter too much what tools are used. Most input devices on tablets (i.e., digitizing pens) closely resemble a pen or pencil, and the more advanced devices allow for pressure sensitivity. Digital drawing devices are evolving to resemble analog drawing materials and methods—the physical act of sketching on a digital device is already very similar to analog sketching, so

Figure I.9   Rocca Minore
Assisi, IT
June 21, 2008
Watercolor on Arches Cold Press paper (9" × 12")
20 minutes

the skills are effectively the same. There are still differences—physical paper has a texture that has yet to be matched in a tablet screen, for example, and physical watercolor still behaves differently than "virtual" watercolor. But digital devices will continue to evolve, in some cases providing new opportunities, but in most cases attempting to replicate existing analog methods for sketching. As this evolution continues, it seems wisest to sketch with whatever materials are handy at the moment. Practicing sketching by hand will build the same skills that might be required to sketch on a digital device. As history has shown, regardless of the device, sketching from observation will always be a valuable practice.

Representation and Abstraction

At the risk of oversimplification, visual art may be representational or abstract—or somewhere in between, as is the case with sketching. Representational art attempts to be clear about its subject, so if an image is intended to depict a tree, it should look enough like a tree that it will not likely be mistaken for anything else.

Figure 1.10 Sunlight Studies, Rua das Portas
Lisbon, PT
July 22, 2011
Derwent Chocolate Pencil on Fabriano Ruvido paper (9" × 12")
3 minutes each

Abstract art may intend to represent a particular subject, but the abstraction opens the work to a variety of interpretations. If the predominant color is green, for example, one observer might interpret the image as a "tree," while another might interpret an implied emotion such as envy. Sketching can be used to explore non-representational subjects, but in sketching on location, the focus is on drawing what we see in an accurate way. Yet it is helpful to understand representation and abstraction if we would like to sketch with some degree of visual accuracy, but without expecting to replicate a subject with photographic precision. While sketching from observation lies somewhere between the two ends of the spectrum, it is generally closer to representation than it is to abstraction.

As I noted previously, representational art has fallen out of favor over the past century or more, having been replaced by a wide variety of abstractions intended to express the mental or emotional state of the artist, or to make statements about society, or merely to compete with other artists. If the abstraction requires lengthy explanation, this is typically seen as a positive. In this context, representational art is sometimes denigrated as being less than serious—a quaint hobby, perhaps, or a type of folk art. Representational art rarely attempts to make philosophical or political statements, but this should not be seen as any sort of failing. There is great value in the simple act of drawing what we see, and in trying to make our drawings clear and accurate enough to convey a view without any explanation. But if a representational sketch is trying to recreate what we see, why not simply take a picture? What is the value in trying to accurately draw a view, rather than interpreting, or drawing an "abstract impression" of what we see? Above all, the value lies in our need to study the subject as it appears. Taking a photograph may require some amount of study, but it is not required—too often, we simply point and shoot without much critical observation. But to draw something accurately, the subject must be studied thoughtfully, for some amount of time. So the value of representational drawing is to be found in our learning about the world. If the resulting images have value, it is usually due to careful study as much as skillful rendering.

Though we may strive to sketch accurately, it is inevitable that a sketch is an interpretation, and some amount of abstraction is unavoidable. Media choices and skill levels are two simple reasons that a sketch will never record a scene as "faithfully" as a camera, but this is also the result of the sketcher's interest in the subject. Some aspects of a view will inevitably be emphasized and others omitted. Too much abstraction, however, leads to a nonrepresentational sketch, perhaps leaving the viewer unclear on the subject matter. Striving for accurate representation in a sketch encourages a sense of responsibility to the subject—there must be enough faithfulness to its geometry and composition, its value and material characteristics, or some combination of these factors. Abstraction, on the other hand, might encourage freedom *from* responsibility in rendering a subject. It can allow for a wider variety of interpretations or emphasis, but it can also lead to sketching without concern for technique. But technique can be learned, and should be learned at every opportunity. It is far better to filter out visual information by choice, rather than doing so for lack of ability. For example, it is better to draw a squiggly line for intended effect, than to make squiggly sketches because one hasn't practiced enough to draw a reasonably straight line. Paradoxically, the more skilled one becomes at making accurate representational sketches, the more likely it is that they will be able to sketch a scene with very few marks—abstraction, but without losing the clarity and accuracy of the subject. This is one of the goals of sketching practice, to find the balance between representation and abstraction. Learning and practicing various techniques is important if the artist is to be prepared for a wide variety of drawing situations and subjects, and desires well-crafted results.

Figure 1.11 Via Sermei
Assisi, IT
June 26, 2011
Derwent Chocolate Pencil on Canson Classic Cream
Drawing paper (9" × 12")
35 minutes

Sketching as a Craft

Sketching on location is a craft that can be acquired by anyone who possesses the physical ability and the desire to learn. Too often, when we see a compelling sketch, the tendency is to back away and say, "Wow, that's amazing, I could never do that!" A much better response would be to get closer to the work and to begin the process of learning how the artist crafted the image. Sketches are never created as if by magic—it only seems that way to someone who hasn't yet learned to sketch well, and who can't conceive of the time and practice required to develop some proficiency. It is easier to ascribe someone else's ability to "talent," as if certain individuals are born with advanced sketching skills. Yet it has been my experience that anyone can learn to draw and constantly improve their skills of observation and representation. And I have yet to encounter someone who was able to draw well without first learning and practicing. What is required is not innate ability, but rather the desire, the patience, and the perseverance to learn. People who seem to possess "talent" are merely those who have taken the time to develop their skills, and to approach their work as a craft.

Craft requires a high degree of care and sustained attention to developing fundamental skills. You must care for the work you are creating, which means avoiding carelessness. Students sometimes approach sketching from the standpoint that a sketch is supposed to look "loose," but this too often translates as "sloppy." While a sketch is most typically created in a short period of time, this should not lead to careless, poorly crafted drawings. Craft requires one to learn and fully acquire technique—not simply to know that certain useful techniques exist, or

Figure 1.12   Ca d'Oro
Venice, IT
July 30, 2009
B and 2B Pencil on on Canson Drawing paper (9" × 12")
120 minutes

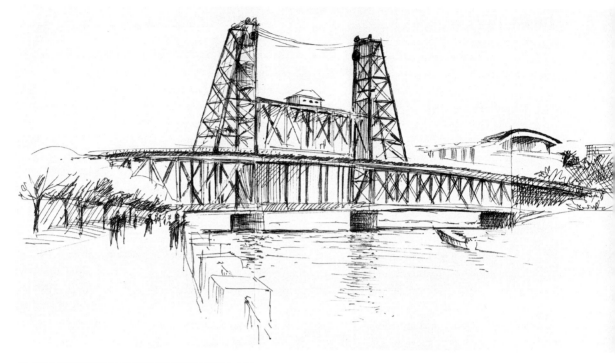

Figure 1.13   Hotel Window
Atrani, IT
June 13, 2010
Watercolor in Moleskine Large Watercolor Sketchbook (5" × 8")
30 minutes

Figure 1.14   Steel Bridge
Portland, OR
October 2, 2010
Uniball Vision Micro Black in Moleskine Large Japanese Notebook (25" × 8")
30 minutes

to try a few new techniques once in a while, but to really adopt as many skills as possible and to be rigorous in their application. It is only after diligent work in building fundamental skills that someone can sketch freely and quickly without being inaccurate or messy.

This book introduces techniques that will lead to the development of sketching as a craft. But reading a book cannot produce the ability to sketch—ability only comes through doing, with concentrated work and much repetition. Making many small drawings is usually better than working for a long time on a single large drawing, but it is very important that the short sketches are not careless sketches. Every sketch is an opportunity to build skills, and to acquire, over time, the ability to become a craftsperson—one who values the quality of what they are making. I've found it helpful to have a subtle, but ever-present, dissatisfaction with my most recent effort. It's not about negating the value of my drawings, but rather acknowledging that I can always do better. In every one of my sketches, I see something to be pleased about, and something that might be improved. It is this dynamic that pushes me forward in my own learning process.

In addition to some of the suggestions made below, in "Learning to Sketch," there are attitudes and habits that will lead to well-crafted sketches. Pay attention to the task, and maintain a strong focus over its duration, whether this is during a series of four-minute practice sketches or during a single sketch that takes an hour to complete. This is the opposite of "multitasking," which is often nothing more than the rapid-fire switching from one activity to another. Care for each step in the process, rather than losing patience and skipping over difficult aspects of a drawing. Be critical of the relative merits of your materials—one type of pencil will be superior to another, for example, based on your experience over time. Always strive to create something of value with your developing skills, and do the best you possibly can in any given situation. These are some of the hallmarks of the craft of sketching.

Learning to Sketch

Sketching is an ongoing practice, as there is always more to learn, and every sketch presents an opportunity to improve. Typically, our attention is focused on the subject we are sketching, and we simply rely on our established abilities to do the drawing. But if our skills are to improve, we must focus frequently on the techniques used to observe and record what we see. Taking drawing classes is certainly a good thing to do, but these are not always available, and they seldom focus specifically on location drawing. To really improve over time, you should develop strategies for learning in the absence of a teacher. A good teacher will not allow a student to skip over the fundamentals of a craft, so you mustn't allow yourself to take shortcuts, either. Keep in mind that learning does not happen overnight, it takes time and much repetition. Learning to sketch is like learning other skills that require knowledge combined with technique—learning to play a musical instrument, for example, or learning to cook well. Such learning involves repetition, attention to the quality of the work, and, above all, a strong focus on the fundamentals. It is only when strong basic skills are established that more advanced work can occur. Drawing itself is best approached as a learning process. Cultivating this attitude as a learner—that is, becoming your own best teacher—will lead to continual improvement in the act of sketching on location.

What follows are some suggestions for initiating and continuing the learning process. Some are general and some are more specific. All are intended to help you develop the habits of someone who is not just sketching a lot, but who is trying to improve and expand their abilities. Drawing often is one of the ways you can grow as a sketcher, but it will not work on its own. If you'd like to improve, you do need to draw frequently, but always with the purpose of learning and improving your skills.

◆ Draw regularly—every day, if possible. It may help to set small, well-defined, achievable goals, such as "three 10-minute sketches, four days each week," or something similar.

◆ Always carry a small sketchbook with you, so you're prepared in case you get stuck in a doctor's waiting room, or you see something particularly sketch-worthy.

◆ Try to avoid frustration. If a sketch doesn't seem to be going well for you, turn the page, look for a different subject, and start a new sketch. Or try the same sketch again, with a different attitude—usually trying the same sketch in a shorter time can help. Probably the worst thing to do is to keep working on a sketch that has become frustrating.

◆ Keep your practice sketches small: 2" × 3" is about right. More frequent, shorter duration sketches are generally better practice than larger, longer, less frequent drawings. With time, your skills will develop, you will be able to observe and sketch more swiftly, and you will be better prepared to make larger sketches without getting bogged down in detail.

◆ Study other people's drawings, and don't be afraid to apply their techniques to your drawings. If you are concerned about "originality," don't worry. Every artist has learned by acquiring techniques from others.

◆ Carry images of sketches you would like to learn from. Keep a few of these in your sketchbook and refer to them when you're actually out there sketching.

◆ Target your weaknesses. It's common for people learning a new skill to do most often the things they already do well. Repeating what you have already mastered can be a good form of practice, but if you only practice the aspects of sketching that feel comfortable, or that you feel are your strengths, your overall improvement will slow down. Focus on aspects that give you trouble—whether it is perspective, or value, or a particular drawing medium such as watercolor.

Figure 1.15   Cathédrale Marie-Reine-du-Monde
Montreal, CA
March 5, 2011
2B Pencil on Canson Drawing paper (9" × 12")
20 minutes

◆ Invite constructive criticism of your drawings, and avoid the tendency to be protective or shy about your work. Share your sketches online and offer your own criticism of your work, which will let others know that you won't take offense if they make helpful suggestions.

◆ Try using media that you haven't used before, or haven't used in some time. If you are "comfortable" with a particular medium, perhaps it's time to try something else for a while, if only to challenge yourself.

These are just a few suggestions for learning—or teaching yourself—how to sketch on location. Try to adopt an ethic of continuous learning, knowing that your skills can always be developed and improved upon. Be creative in your methods for teaching yourself, be open to receiving assistance from others, and be generous in assisting your fellow sketchers. Teaching and learning comprise a general attitude toward a particular skill or craft, and both need to be present in order to build a comprehensive approach to the craft of sketching on location. Keep these bits of advice in mind as you begin to sketch, and as your abilities grow over time.

Figure 1.16   Praça do Comércio
Lisbon, PT
July 23, 2011
Watercolor in Moleskine Large Watercolor Sketchbook (16" × 5")
45 minutes

HALF PRICE BOOKS ®

Half Price Books
1835 Forms Drive
Carrollton, TX 75006
OFS OrderID 22994608

‖‖‖‖‖‖‖ ‖‖ ‖‖‖‖

Thank you for your order, Wendy Lunardi!

Thank you for shopping with Half Price Books! Please contact Support@hpb.com. if you have any
questions, comments or concerns about your order (112-9822563-9612204)

Visit our stores to sell your books, music, movies games for cash.

SKU	ISBN/UPC	Title & Author/Artist	Shelf ID	Qty	OrderSKU
S343329756	9781465205261	Sketching on Location Matthew Brehm	65--15--2	1	‖‖‖‖‖‖‖

SHIPPED STANDARD TO:
Wendy Lunardi
6683 OLDE EIGHT RD
PENINSULA OH 44264-9744
7vy65nsgwj45ys2@marketplace.amazon.com

ORDER# 112-9822563-9612204
AmazonMarketplaceUS

CHAPTER

2   *MATERIALS*

A simple pencil or pen, and ordinary paper—this is all that's really necessary to begin sketching. As you learn to sketch more effectively, and make it a regular activity, the type and quality of your materials will become more important. But the lack of "proper" materials should never stop you from sketching. There's not much sense in being too selective about materials, especially if you are just beginning to sketch. It's far more important to sketch as often as possible, no matter what materials happen to be within reach. In fact, it is often the times when your favored materials are not close at hand that you can have interesting and worthwhile sketching experiences. A paper tablecloth in a restaurant, for example, can be an opportunity to observe one's surroundings while waiting for food to arrive.

Selecting Sketching Materials

As you develop some experience with various sketching materials, you will likely become more selective based on what works for you. Your preference for wet or dry media, the particular subjects you find interesting, or your willingness to carry a lot of gear (or your lack of willingness)—these are some of the issues that will influence your choice of sketching materials. As a general approach, try to balance the following factors.

Quality

Always try to select and purchase the best quality materials available. The best quality doesn't necessarily mean the most expensive, it just means what works best for your purposes. One of the most appealing aspects of sketching is that the required materials are relatively inexpensive, and that these materials can be used to create images of real and lasting value. The sketches will certainly be valuable in themselves, if only to the sketcher. But, more importantly, sketches are the tangible evidence of an intangible learning process. Having observed one's surroundings with a critical and attentive eye, and having processed what one sees into a sketch, is priceless—and far more valuable than the worth of any single drawing. Nevertheless, with time, your sketches and sketchbooks will almost certainly become more valuable to you. If you use materials of poor quality, the sketches you make might not last very long—they may fade or change color, for example—so always use the highest-quality materials available.

Consistency

To develop mastery with any medium, you must spend time working with it. If you constantly shift from one medium to another, it will be difficult to learn about the capabilities of any particular one, and your skills with that medium will be slow to develop as well. Spend time—perhaps a month or two, maybe even longer—working only in graphite, then move on to ink for a similar amount of time, then watercolor, etc. Really strive to build your skill with that single medium, and don't worry if you're not paying any attention to other media types for a while. It does make sense to try a variety of brands within the scope of one medium—trying a few of different brands of pen, for example, will help you to know what's available and what might work best for you. Testing how various papers respond to a single medium is also very worthwhile, but it is only after consistently using a particular medium that you will thoroughly understand its capabilities and its limitations.

Variety

Though this may seem to contradict the idea of "consistency," it is important to experiment occasionally with new media types, and to develop some mastery with at least a few. In other words, try to avoid getting locked-in to using only a single media type for extended periods. There are times when a particular subject calls for a particular medium, or combination of media, and it's best to be prepared. For example, a brightly colored scene might suggest watercolor, a more rigorous architectural subject might call for pen, or a richly textured landscape view might best be rendered in graphite. Or, you might simply be in a "pencil mood," or perhaps you haven't used watercolor for some time. In any event, try to balance the need for consistency, as discussed above, with the need to keep yourself challenged and prepared for a variety of sketching situations.

With these factors in mind, what follows are recommendations for basic sketching materials. It is not intended to be a comprehensive list—there are many other materials that might be effectively used for sketching. Nor is it intended to be a list of required materials necessary to begin sketching—remember, all that is really needed to sketch is a simple pencil or pen and ordinary paper. Rather, these suggestions will hopefully serve as a guide as you begin to develop your sketching skills, and as the type and quality of materials becomes more important to you.

Paper

There is great variety in the type of paper that can be used for sketching, and certain drawing instruments will perform much more effectively on some papers rather than others. Generally, smoother paper is more appropriate for pen and ink, while paper with some "tooth" (i.e., a slightly textured surface) works best with pencil and other dry media, and watercolor certainly works best with paper made specifically for that medium. Experimentation can yield interesting results, however, so try not to be overly particular about matching certain papers with certain media. What follows are some suggestions based on my experience.

For pencil and charcoal sketching, I prefer a medium texture paper. Canson "Drawing" paper is an excellent choice, and it comes in pads in a variety of sizes. The paper can be purchased in different tones, with "Classic Cream" being my personal favorite. The off-white tone of this paper works very well with graphite, charcoal, and colored pencils.

For sketching in pen, a smoother paper is desirable to avoid "feathering" (i.e., fuzzy lines that result from ink spreading into the paper fiber). But paper that is too smooth may be problematic as well—certain types of ink may not be absorbed quickly, leading to lines that are easily smudged or smeared before the sketch is complete. Bristol is a type of paper with a smooth surface that is perfect for pen sketches. It is generally available with either a "Plate" surface (very smooth), or a "Vellum" surface (with a bit of texture). Both surfaces work well with most pens. The paper in the standard Moleskine sketchbook is very smooth, almost slick, and works very well with felt- or fiber-tipped pens, and pens that contain a quick-drying, water-resistant ink. Water-soluble inks, and inks that are slow to dry, tend to bead-up on this type of paper. The result is that lines smear easily, and small drops of wet ink can be transferred to the facing page if the sketchbook is closed before the ink is completely dry.

With regard to watercolor paper, there are many options regarding price, quality, and format. A simple pad of "watercolor paper" can work well if the paper is thick enough to resist buckling when water is applied. A "watercolor block" with gum around all four sides will work better, but these can be expensive and they have their own limitations—for example, they tend to be heavier than an ordinary pad or ring-bound book. Moleskine makes watercolor sketchbooks with high-quality paper that is thick enough to keep from buckling too much. Regarding the various surfaces available, "Rough" is just what it says, while "Hot Press" has a smooth surface, and "Cold Press" is somewhere between these two. For general outdoor sketching/painting, a block, pad or sketchbook of Cold Press works very well. Arches Cold Press pads are an excellent solution—very high quality paper without the expense of a block.

Sketchbooks

It seems there are always new sketchbooks appearing on the market, and it can be difficult to decide which sketchbook will suit your purposes. As with all sketching media, it is worthwhile to experiment. It is not always possible to find your preferred paper type in a sketchbook that matches your preferred format. If you like to sketch with a variety of media, and in a variety of formats, the only practical solution may be to use several sketchbooks at once. If this isn't acceptable, you may choose to construct your own sketchbooks, allowing you to determine the exact paper type, binding, and format for your needs.

Figure 2.1   A variety of recommended sketchbook formats, types, and sizes. The two on the right are hardcover books, with paper suitable for watercolor.

When purchasing a sketchbook, the primary factors to be considered are: size, format, paper, and durability. Smaller sketchbooks are more portable, but I wouldn't recommend using a sketchbook that is less than 5" in its smallest dimension, especially when you are just getting started. "Format" refers to the orientation of the book—Portrait (with a longer vertical dimension), Landscape (with a longer horizontal dimension), or Square. Of course, a Portrait or Landscape sketchbook may be turned ninety degrees and used for a different orientation. But when a Landscape book is held open, its long dimension is usually very long. This offers interesting opportunities for sketching extremely horizontal or vertical subjects, but if you like to write journal passages in your sketchbooks, writing in a Landscape book can be considerably less comfortable than in a Portrait book.

I recommend that beginners start with an inexpensive ring-bound sketchbook with all-purpose paper. Aquabee "Super Deluxe," Legion Paper "Stonehenge," and Strathmore "Sketch" are all good choices, and are available in a few sizes and formats. An advantage of a ring-bound format is that the book can be completely opened, with the front cover turned against the back, making the book comfortable to hold while sketching. Some books of this type are equipped with perforated pages, so that individual sketches can be cleanly removed for framing or other purposes. I recommend a square format, because it does not favor either a vertical or horizontal orientation, allowing more freedom in terms of sketch composition. A sketchbook sized 7" × 7" or 9" × 9" will be ideal.

Don't be concerned if you don't completely fill every sketchbook, especially the first few sketchbooks you use. It's probably better to move on to a new sketchbook once in a while, if only to try a different format or a new type of paper. In fact, because there is such variety in sketchbook types and formats, it may be a good strategy to work with several sketchbooks at once. Occasionally, I use one sketchbook for a particular theme—for example, I have one book that contains only sketches from the University of Oregon campus, where I studied and taught architecture from 1993 until 2004, and another for the University of Idaho campus, where I began teaching in 2004.

Sometimes, I feel that working in a sketchbook can be too confining—perhaps I'd like to work on a larger size paper, but would rather not carry a large book, or I'd like to make sketches that are suitable for framing without having to tear pages out of a sketchbook. At these times, I work with pads of paper. These can be similar to ring-bound sketchbooks with perforated pages, or they might have a gummed edge. I regularly use pads of Canson 9" × 12" Classic Cream paper for pencil and charcoal sketches, and pads of Arches 9" × 12" Cold Press for watercolors. In either case, the page can be cleanly removed and placed in a portfolio for protection until it's time for framing. The Itoya "Profolio" is a type of portfolio with clear sleeves that is available in various sizes, and is perfect for this purpose.

Pencils

When we use the word "pencil," we are most often talking about graphite encased in wood. There are other types of pencil that are very effective for sketching, such as colored pencils and charcoal pencils. But the basic graphite pencil is a tried and true drawing instrument, and developing strong skills in graphite can form a solid foundation for sketching with other media. My preferred brand of graphite pencil is the Staedtler-Mars "Lumograph," which is consistently smooth and free of grit. Faber-Castell is another excellent brand.

There are several grades of graphite, based on density (hard vs. soft) and color (gray vs. black). 9H is typically the hardest grade available, and as the number lowers, so does the hardness, such that an H (the number 1 is usually left out) is the softest of the H-graded pencils. HB is at the center of the density scale, and roughly corresponds in density to the ubiquitous No. 2 pencil. As the numbers increase on the B-side of the scale, the softness of the graphite increases, such that 9B is typically the softest graphite available. The hardest graphite allows for clean, dust-free sketches, and relatively precise lines. However, sketching with hard

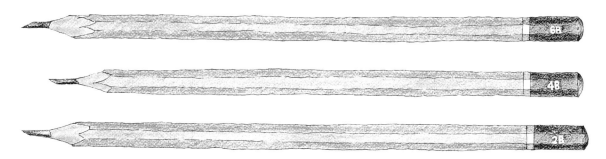

Figure 2.2   Graphite pencils in three grades of softness appropriate for sketching.

graphite makes it difficult to create strong, legible marks on the page without marring the paper surface. The softest graphite can create rich dark tones, much like charcoal, but it can also smudge very easily, sometimes leading to muddy, imprecise sketches. Therefore, it is best to strike a balance between hard and soft graphite.

As seen in the image, the graphite toward the hard (H) end of the scale becomes rather difficult to see, and no matter how firmly one presses on the page, the pencil can only produce a very limited value of gray. Toward the soft (B) end of the scale, the graphite becomes so soft that it is difficult to draw a clear line or to keep the tip reasonably sharp. The colors of graphite also vary significantly—pencils from 2H through 9H are typically very light gray, while pencils from 5B through 9B can be very dark black, similar to charcoal. To prevent color contrast when using more than one grade of graphite in a single sketch, it is best to use pencils that are adjacent on the scale, with no more than three or four grades of difference between them. In the majority of my pencil-sketching work, I try to use a single pencil. If I use more than one, it would be an HB or B for the setup, and a 2B or 4B for value. With slightly harder graphite, I am able to lay down thin, light setup lines that tend to disappear as value is added to the sketch with one or more softer pencils. With slightly softer graphite, I am able to lay down rich, dark tones for shading. Each person will find their own favored grades of graphite, but I would recommend starting at the center of the scale and then working into the B-range. With anything harder than a 2H, it is very difficult to get truly dark tones, and with anything softer than a 4B, it becomes difficult to make very light lines, and to keep the sketch clean and free of graphite dust and smudges. By focusing on the graphite scale between 2H and 4B, you will develop a sense of pressure (or "touch") that allows for faint lines with relatively soft graphite. This approach will reduce the need to use multiple grades of graphite, and simplify the process of sketching with pencils.

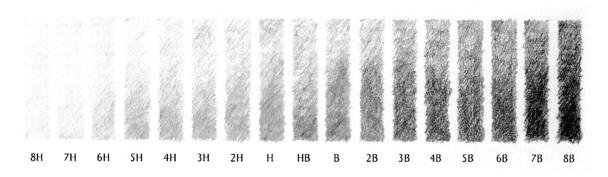

Figure 2.3   Graphite scale, with the hardest/lightest graphite at left, and the softest/darkest at right. Any grades may be used for sketching, but the most suitable range from H to 4B.

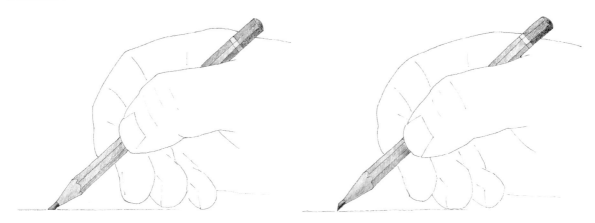

Figure 2.4   Pencil point with one side sanded down, allowing for broad strokes (left) and fine lines (right).

An advantage of using a wooden pencil is the variety of line "weights" (i.e., thicknesses) possible from a single instrument. A simple sharpening technique makes this possible. A finely sharpened pencil will work well, especially for the initial light lines made during the setup. But if the graphite is of a soft grade, the pencil will lose its point fairly rapidly. Rather than using a conventional pencil sharpener, try using a small pocket knife to shave away enough wood to expose about 3/8" of the lead. Then, using a sandpaper block or a blank sheet of paper, wear the point down while holding the pencil at about a 45-degree angle. Thin lines may then be made with the sharper tip of the lead, while broad strokes can be produced with the flattened portion of the graphite. For squared strokes, the tip may be worn down to produce a straight and flat end to the point. Experiment with various sharpening techniques to get the maximum versatility out of a single pencil.

Charcoal

Charcoal pencils make for a worthwhile change of pace from graphite, but they are a bit more challenging. Because of its dusty consistency, charcoal requires more care in keeping the sketch clean, but it is far easier to produce rich, dark values with charcoal than with graphite. Charcoal pencils are typically available in three grades of density—hard (which is similar to HB on the graphite scale), medium (2B), and soft (4B). The most important characteristic in selecting a brand is the smoothness of the charcoal—it should be as free of grit as possible. Of the brands available, I have found General's Charcoal to be the most consistently smooth.

Figure 2.5   Charcoal pencils with wood casing are cleaner to work with and more precise than vine or willow charcoal.

Colored Pencils

Colored pencils may be used individually, for a monochromatic sketch, or in combination, by mixing various colors on the page. When using a single color, I have enjoyed the results of earth tones such as Derwent's "Venetian Red" (similar to Burnt Umber), or "Chocolate" (a dark Sepia). Any relatively dark color is worth trying. It is not often practical to carry a large number of colored pencils when sketching on location, so it is important to learn how to mix colors. This will be covered in detail in the chapter titled "Color." For now, it will suffice to

Figure 2.6   Colored pencils (top to bottom): Prismacolor Magenta, True Blue, and Canary Yellow; Derwent Venetian Red and Chocolate.

say that sketching in colored pencil only requires the three primary colors. The most widely available brand of colored pencil is Prismacolor, and within this brand the three basic primaries are most commonly understood to be "Canary Yellow," "True Blue," and "Magenta."

Pen and Ink

The ordinary ballpoint pen is perhaps the most readily available sketching tool, but it is worthwhile to try a variety of pens before settling on one or a few types that work well for you. There are three basic types of pen that can be used for sketching. First, there are the disposable ink pens—ballpoint, rolling ball, and gel pens are in this category. Second are the disposable felt- or fiber-tipped pens, which are essentially like markers, but with finer points. Third are the refillable pens—fountain pens, technical pens, and quill pens come under this group. Each type of pen has its advantages and disadvantages, particularly when it comes to combining an ink sketch with other media such as watercolor.

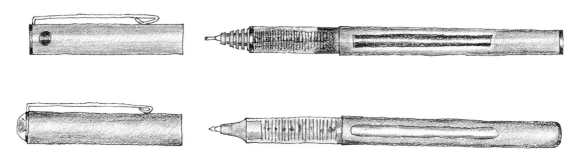

Figure 2.7   Rolling ball pens: Pilot Precise V5 Black (top) and Uniball Vision Micro Blue (bottom).

While the ballpoint pen is an acceptable sketching instrument, it doesn't always provide a precise or consistent line. Rolling ball pens and gel pens are superior in this regard. Uniball, Pilot, and Staedtler-Mars all produce excellent pens, with precise and consistent line quality. The available ink colors are somewhat limited, however, with black, blue, and red being the most common. Most rolling ball and gel pens are at least somewhat water resistant, making them suitable for use with watercolor, but individual pen types should be tested for this characteristic.

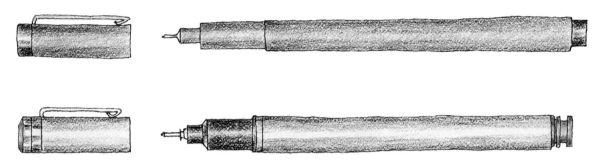

Figure 2.8   Felt-tip pens: Staedtler Pigment Liner Black (top) and Copic Multiliner SP Sepia (bottom).

Felt-tip pens are available in many sizes, and while black is the most widely available ink color, some companies (such as Copic) offer more variety. In almost all cases, felt-tip pens are disposable. When the ink runs out or the tip (also known as the "nib") becomes deformed, the pen must be thrown away. One notable exception is the Copic Multiliner SP, which has a replaceable nib and refillable cartridges. Most felt-tipped pens contain ink that is water resistant, and some are fully waterproof—making this type of pen an excellent choice for use with watercolor. These pens are often available in a variety of sizes, from very fine points to wide tips or even brushlike tips. The Faber-Castell Pitt Artist pen is available in a variety of colors and nib sizes.

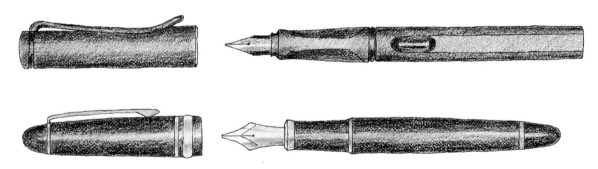

Figure 2.9   Fountain pens: Lamy Safari (top) and Yafa Iridium (bottom).

Fountain pens offer many advantages, foremost being their variable line quality and their ability to use a wide variety of inks. Though the initial cost is considerably higher than that of disposable pens, fountain pens last for years if they are well cared for, and they even adapt over time to the particular hand of the owner. All fountain pens require special care in their use and handling—if a fountain pen is dropped or bumped, it's very likely that ink will leak or splatter from the nib. They must be maintained through occasional cleaning, by flushing with cool water in between ink refills. There is an enormous variety of inks that can be used with fountain pens—different colors and levels of permanence—but all fountain pen inks must be water soluble to some extent, or they will not flow properly and perhaps cause clogging in the feed or nib. So if watercolor is to be added to a fountain pen sketch, some bleeding of the ink on the page is to be expected. This can contribute to interesting effects, but there are some inks specially formulated to resist bleeding more than others. Most fountain pens can be "refilled" by changing a disposable cartridge. These cartridges are sold by the pen manufacturer, and the choices of ink are typically limited. Better pens will usually include a refillable reservoir for the ink, called a *converter*, which allows for a greater variety of ink types and colors to be used in the pen. Fountain pen nibs are made of steel or gold. Gold is understandably more expensive, but it is generally more flexible and more durable over the life of the pen. Nibs vary in size, from fine to wide, and they also vary in flexibility, from quite stiff to almost springlike. A medium- or fine-pointed, semiflexible nib is a good place to start when selecting a fountain pen. All nibs can produce a variable line thickness, depending on the pressure applied—more pressure will create a wider line, but be aware that too much pressure can damage the nib. One of the most affordable—and yet durable—fountain pens on the market is the Lamy Safari. These pens are readily available at many stationery and art supply stores.

Watercolor

As with pens, there is great variety and many levels of quality to choose from when shopping for watercolor supplies. Try to start simple, with only the basic necessities: a palette with a few (primary) colors, and a brush. By keeping the kit small, it is easier to justify spending the money for high-quality materials that will work well and last a long time. As your skill and interest grow, you can add to the kit a little at a time while maintaining high quality.

Brushes

Brushes can be very expensive, and can come in a dizzying array of shapes and types. As with all sketching materials, you should buy the very best you can afford. If a brush is well made and cared for properly, it will last a lifetime. If the brush is cheap, it's more likely that it will perform poorly and fall apart too soon. The fibers of a good brush will be flexible, and thus able to hold a fair amount of water, without losing their shape. Real Sable brushes are the best, but they can be prohibitively expensive. Synthetic Sable brushes offer a good compromise between quality and price, and are what I would recommend, especially for beginners. Taklon brushes (with white synthetic fibers) also seem to work fairly well for the price. I usually just work with a single

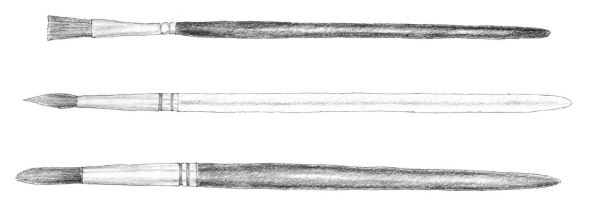

Figure 2.10   Watercolor brushes (top to bottom): Princeton Synthetic Sable ¼" Flat, Connoisseur Kolinski Sable Round #6, Blick Scholastic Red Sable #10.

#6 Round brush, to keep things simple. If you are doing larger work, a #10 or #12 will be worth having. I don't have a strong preference for a particular brand, but I currently have a Princeton Synthetic Sable #6 Round, a Connoisseur Kolinski Sable #6 Round, and a Blick Red Sable #10 Round. Brushes with exceptionally long handles are best for work in the studio, and are less effective when sketching on location. In order to make long-handled brushes more portable, I have cut the handles down to size so they will fit in a carrying case. Never leave a watercolor brush standing with its bristles down in a container of water for any length of time—the fibers may deform and the brush will be ruined. Also, avoid using hot water to clean the brush, and never pull on the bristles.

Another option is the "waterbrush." This is a brush that has an integrated container or cartridge of water, which is squeezed to inject the water into the brush fibers. The advantages are that they make a separate water reservoir unnecessary, and that they can be filled with premixed color for consistent monochromatic washes. They are a great option if portability is a primary concern. The disadvantage is that there is a strong tendency to draw with the brush, rather than using the water to distribute the pigment, and the ratio of water to pigment cannot be held constant, which means that large areas cannot be painted as consistently as would be possible with an ordinary brush. Waterbrushes can be very effective for small, on-the-go sketches, but they are not recommended for larger sketches, or for learning how to work with watercolors as a medium.

Colors

Use the best colors you can afford, and be sure to buy tubes as opposed to dry pigments. Tubes of wet color are much easier to use and mix, and it's easier to expand your palette a few tubes at a time. Dry colors that are often found in starter's sets can make it difficult to use and mix the proper amount of pigment. Poor quality colors may not mix well and tend to fade over time. M. Graham & Co. is the best brand that I've found—excellent colors at reasonable prices. Start with these three primary colors and then gradually expand your palette with other colors as needed: Cerulean Blue, Cadmium Yellow Light, Cadmium Red. With these three colors (or similar versions of Blue, Yellow, and Red), practice mixing secondary colors, involving two of the primaries, and tertiary colors, involving all three primaries. It is best to practice mixing colors as much as possible, for as long as possible, with only the three primaries, before expanding the palette with additional colors. Eventually, adding colors to the palette will create new opportunities for color mixing. An initial expansion of the palette would logically include alternatives to the primary colors, such as Alizarin Crimson, Gamboge, Ultramarine Blue. A further expansion of the palette might be focused on greens and earth tones: Hooker's Green, Raw Sienna, Burnt Sienna, Yellow Ochre, Sepia, etc. Personally, I limit my palette to twelve colors at a time—if I would like to add a new color, I'm forced to eliminate another. This strategy keeps my palette simple and makes me consider the colors carefully.

Palette

Try to find a small, durable travel palette. Plastic palettes are the most widely available, but I prefer one made of metal, with a white enameled interior and plenty of spaces to deposit colors. Having a thumb grip is useful, but it might not be essential if the palette is easy to hold with one hand. It's also good to have a palette that's easy to clean, so keep that in mind while you're shopping. The Martin brand Universal Design Metal Palette is a good option.

Small starter's sets (which include a palette, colors, and perhaps a small brush) can seem to be a good value, but they sometimes contain components (colors or brush) that are of inferior quality. It is best to purchase individual components—even if you buy high-quality colors and a high-quality brush, the total cost will be comparable or even a bit less than the cost of a watercolor kit.

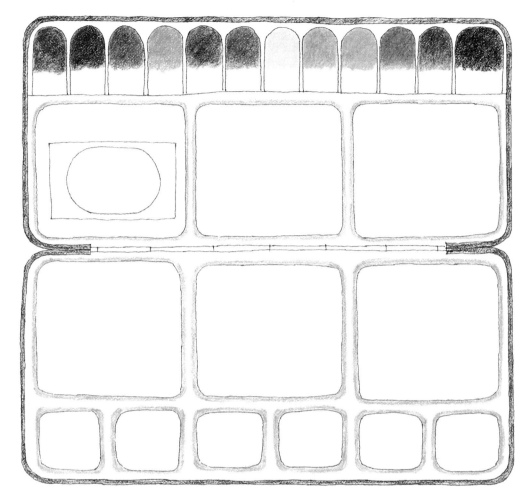

Figure 2.11   Watercolor palette, with colors from M. Graham & Co. (left to right): Cadmium Red, Alizarin Crimson, Ultramarine Blue, Cerulean Blue, Prussian Blue, Hooker's Green, Cadmium Yellow Light, Gamboge, Yellow Ochre, Raw Sienna, Burnt Sienna, and Sepia.

Accessories

There are numerous accessories that can be useful for sketching. Some are essential to carry at all times, while others might be considered a luxury. A stool, for example, is something many sketchers would not do without, but I've never bothered to carry one in all my years of sketching. To me, even the most compact, collapsible stools represent added bulk and weight when I'm traveling or just sketching around town, and when I really need to sit down, it has never a problem to find a suitable bench, a low wall, or some stairs. Other accessories are not so large, and you will decide for yourself which are essential and which can be omitted from your list.

♦   **Erasers:** as discussed in the chapter titled "Getting Started," I don't advocate the regular use of erasers. But it's good to carry one for cleaning up smudges on the page. White plastic erasers are good for erasing significant marks, and kneaded erasers are perfect for lifting charcoal smudges.

♦   **Pocket Knife:** an excellent tool for sharpening wood pencils or cutting sheets from a watercolor block. Just be careful not to pack a knife in your carry-on bag when you fly—it will likely be confiscated by security.

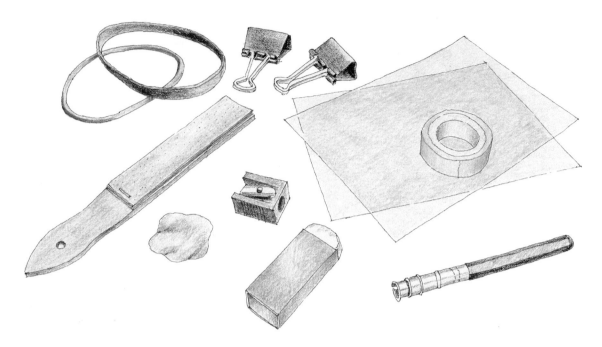

Figure 2.12   Accessories (clockwise from lower right): Pencil extender, white plastic eraser, pencil sharpener, kneaded eraser, sandpaper block, rubber bands, binder clips, trace paper sheets, and drafting tape.

- **Pocket Pencil Sharpener:** although a pocket knife will work better, a pencil sharpener is unlikely to be confiscated when you fly.

- **Sandpaper Block:** available at most art stores, a sandpaper block is a great tool for shaping the tip of a graphite or charcoal pencil. Not an essential accessory—pencils may be shaped just as easily by rubbing on a blank page, or on the sidewalk—but it is perfect for this purpose.

- **Pencil Case:** a single bag or small box in which to carry all your gear. Keep it small, so you're more likely to carry it with you wherever you go, and so that you're not tempted to carry all of your gear all of the time.

- **Small Sheets of Trace Paper:** for protecting sketches in dry media from smudging in sketchbooks.

- **Drafting Tape:** not an essential accessory, but a small roll of drafting tape can be useful, especially for masking watercolor sketches. Tape can also be used to secure sheets of trace paper over graphite or charcoal. Drafting tape is preferable—masking tape is more likely to damage the surface of most types of sketching paper.

- **Glue Stick:** not essential, but can be handy for pasting mementos in a sketchbook, such as tickets, receipts, and other items that help tell the story of where a sketch was made.

- **Pencil Extender:** a wood and metal device that greatly extends the life and value of your pencils. Because I so often sketch with pencil, I think of these as being essential accessories.

- **Rubber Bands and/or Binder Clips:** these are sometimes handy to hold sketchbook pages down on a windy day. They are also good for holding a sketchbook or pad of paper closed so that pages are less likely to rub together, thus preventing graphite and charcoal sketches from smudging.

- **Water Reservoir:** essential gear for watercolor. Any basic cup and/or bottle with a wide opening will work fine.

- **Paper Towels:** also essential for watercolor. A few sheets folded up and carried in the palette will keep you prepared for spills or mistakes.

SKETCHING SUPPLY LIST

Tear out this page and carry it with you to the art supply store. Use it as a reminder or simplified guide to the materials and issues discussed in this chapter.

With regard to sketching materials, try to balance these factors:

♦ **Quality**—always purchase the best quality materials you can afford.
♦ **Consistency**—spend the necessary time with each medium until you develop your skills.
♦ **Variety**—mix things up on occasion, try something new, consider the relationship between subject and media.

Papers and Sketchbooks

Drawing papers for pencil and other dry media should have some "tooth" or texture.

Recommended:

❑ Canson "Artist's Series" Drawing Pads
❑ Strathmore "Sketch 400 Series" Sketchbooks
❑ Aquabee "Super Deluxe" Sketchbooks
❑ Moleskine Sketchbooks and Watercolor Sketchbooks

Watercolor Papers:

❑ Rough
❑ Cold Press (recommended for all-purpose watercolor sketching)
❑ Hot Press

Pencils

Recommended (in grades from 2H to 4B):

❑ Staedtler "Mars Lumograph"
❑ Derwent "Sketching" (graphite)
❑ Derwent "Drawing" (colors: Chocolate, Venetian Red, Terra Cotta)
❑ General's "Charcoal"

❑ Sanford "Draughting" and "Design Ebony"

❑ Sanford "Prismacolor" (colors: start with True Blue, Magenta, Canary Yellow)

❑ Pitt "Oil Base"

Pens

Recommended:

❑ Uniball "Vision Series"

❑ Pilot "Precise V5"

❑ Faber-Castell "Pitt Artist Pen"

❑ Copic "Multiliner" and "Multiliner SP"

❑ Staedtler "Liquid Point"

Watercolors

Recommended:

❑ M.Graham "Artists' Watercolor" tubes

❑ Winsor & Newton "Artists' Water Colour" tubes

◆ **Primary Colors:** Cerulean Blue, Cadmium Yellow Light, Cadmium Red
◆ **Alternate "Primary" Colors:** Alizarin Crimson, Gamboge, Ultramarine Blue
◆ **Optional Colors to Expand the Palette:** Hooker's Green, Raw Sienna, Burnt Sienna, Yellow Ochre, Sepia

Accessories

❑ Erasers

❑ Pocket knife

❑ Pocket pencil sharpener

❑ Sandpaper block

❑ Pencil case

❑ Small sheets of trace paper

❑ Drafting tape

❑ Glue stick

❑ Pencil extender

❑ Rubber bands and/or binder clips

❑ Water reservoir

❑ Paper towels

CHAPTER

3 *GETTING STARTED*

The process of sketching can be as simple as looking at a subject and drawing what you see, but there are several techniques and strategies that can be helpful when you are just beginning to make a sketch. Of course, not all of these need to be used on every sketch—the more skill you develop in applying various methods, the more comfortable you will become in using specific techniques when the need arises. Learning to sketch is very similar to learning any skill requiring knowledge and dexterity, such as the ability to play a musical instrument. It will likely feel somewhat unnatural at first, and it may seem like there is an impossible amount to learn. But with diligent practice, it will begin to feel more comfortable and natural. Your ability to process visual information will increase, and your hands will become more able to make the marks that your eyes and brain are telling them to make. So don't worry about memorizing all of the points and techniques that are presented here, and don't feel as if you have to use every technique for every sketch. Take some time initially to learn and acquire these skills, and then keep practicing even as you become more comfortable with sketching on location.

Basic Techniques

Over time, and with concentrated practice, each individual will develop their own ways of making marks on the page. Some sketchers hold the pencil or pen in highly unorthodox ways, but are no less effective. However, there are some general strategies that will assist the beginner, and it is best to develop good habits from

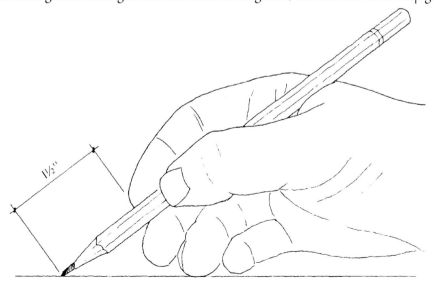

Figure 3.1   Hold the pen, pencil, or brush firmly but not tightly, with your fingers about 1½" from the tip.

the start. Hold the pen or pencil firmly, but not tightly. If your hand begins to cramp or get sore after 10 or 15 minutes of sketching, your grip is too tight. Avoid holding the pen or pencil too close to the tip—there should be approximately 1½" between your fingertips and the point. Your hand should be relaxed but still able to control the point. For shorter or more precise strokes, your fingers will do most of the work, but for more broad or lengthy strokes, keep the fingers in a steady position and move your wrist or your forearm for the best results. Don't anchor your hand to the page too firmly, as this will prevent you from drawing effectively with your wrist or arm.

Practice making a wide variety of marks on the page. Use an inexpensive sketchbook and fill many pages with lines and patterns. It is usually most comfortable to make something resembling 45-degree lines, as this is the dominant pattern for handwriting, but you should practice making swift lines in every direction until it feels natural. Repeat lines side by side, trying to maintain consistent line quality and spacing. When numerous lines are drawn this way (side by side, and evenly-spaced) it is called a *hatch* pattern. When two or more hatch patterns overlay one another, at opposing angles, it is called a *cross-hatch* pattern. The process of laying down one hatch pattern on top of another is commonly referred to as *building tone*, and is an essential technique for creating value (darkness) on the page. This technique is very useful when sketching with pencil, and it is invaluable with pen and ink. Making hatch patterns can be a relatively loose operation, where each line doesn't need to be so perfectly drawn. Consistency is more important, and this can usually be achieved with swift strokes in the same direction—moving the wrist or forearm, rather than the fingers—but it does require quite a bit of practice over time.

Figure 3.2 Practice marks with a pen. Strive for consistency, especially with hatch and cross-hatch patterns.

Figure 3.3   Sketch showing extensive use of hatch and cross-hatch patterns to build up value.
Quick Care Office
Moscow, ID
January 7, 2009
Copic Multiliner SP (Olive)
Small Moleskine Sketchbook

The ability to make reasonably straight lines is an important skill, but perfectly straight lines are unnecessary for sketching. It's not advisable to use straight edges or rulers—these devices make the process more cumbersome and they often result in lines that lack energy and subtle variation. Nor should you ever use a back-and-forth motion to "sketch" a line—this approach only creates fuzzy, hesitant, unclear marks on the page. The lines you make should be as clear, confident, and smooth as possible. The speed used to make a line has an effect on the result—generally, the more swiftly you make a line, the straighter it will be. When a long straight line is desired, it's most effective to use your arm more than your wrist to make the motion, and again, much practice is needed to develop this skill. But there are other techniques that can help to form reasonably straight lines while sketching. One approach is to put faint points on the page, spaced out evenly along the length of the intended line. Using these points as a guide, draw the line smoothly through the points. Another technique is to put the pencil or pen on the paper at the starting point, and then, while looking at the intended finishing point, draw the line as smoothly and swiftly as possible.

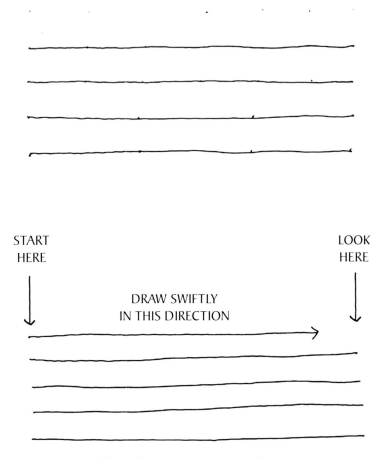

Figure 3.4 Reasonably straight lines can be created by placing points on the page and connecting the dots (top). A faster way to create straight lines is to swiftly draw the line while looking at the intended finish point (bottom).

Sighting and Measuring Techniques

Just as perfectly straight lines are of no use in a sketch, precise measurements are likewise unnecessary. However, the ability to observe and record approximate dimensions is extremely important. The process of observing and recording requires patience and practice, but there are several simple techniques that make the process quicker and the results more accurate. It's more about repeated approximation—bringing the initial, tentative lines and marks toward cohesion—employing whatever strategies might help along the way, rather than striving for immediate precision. The first marks are estimations, which may require correction as more visual information is added to the sketch. At some point during the sketch, enough of the image will have been worked out that additional measuring will become superfluous. In any case, try not to be a slave to the measuring process, and always maintain some flexibility and looseness. If you try to measure everything—every door or window frame, every automobile or person within view—then the act of sketching will become a tedious, lengthy endeavor. As with many aspects of sketching, it's a balancing act between accuracy and expression, between patience and immediacy. Using the following techniques will help you create sketches that are representative of their subjects, but a little can go a long way. Strive to integrate these techniques into your process, but only as much as is required to develop accurate sketches.

◆   **Hand-Framing:** A very simple way to envision potential subjects is to use your hands as a frame. Though this technique is imprecise, and shouldn't be used for measuring, it can be used as a quick method for considering possible sketch compositions. While keeping one eye closed, hold your hands as shown in Figure 3.5, and move them closer to or further from your open eye. It's easiest, and most comfortable, to use this technique for horizontal orientations, but it can also be used for vertical views.

Figure 3.5   Hand-framing can be helpful when you are trying to identify potential subjects for a sketch. (Art & Architecture South Building, University of Idaho; Moscow, ID.)

♦ **Viewfinder:** Using a viewfinder is similar to hand-framing, but with a device that will give more precise results. You can create your own viewfinder, using card stock or thin cardboard, or you can use an empty 35-mm slide frame. It helps if there are tick marks along the edges of the window at the 1/4 and 1/3 points all the way around. These marks can be used as an effective guide as the sketch progresses through the compositional stages of setup (Chapter 4).

Figure 3.6   Using a viewfinder to identify sketching subjects and to help estimate relative proportions of objects in the view. (Via della Lungaretta; Rome, IT.)

◆   **Sight-Sizing:** This technique is taken from academic drawing, where the viewed subject and the drawing are arranged to make them appear at the same size from the point of view of the artist. In sketching, Sight-sizing can be as simple as holding the sketchbook at eye level and comparing the developing sketch to the subject. Doing this repeatedly during the initial setup will help ensure accurate composition, proportion, and perspective (Chapter 4).

Figure 3.7   Using sight-sizing to compare the sketch to the subject. (Vicolo della Moretta; Rome, IT.)

◆   **Pencil-Sighting:** This entails using your pencil or other drawing instrument as a measuring tool, and can be accomplished in two ways. First, for measuring angles, hold the pencil either horizontally or vertically, next to the angle you are trying to find. Look at the angle formed between the pencil and the subject. This will help establish the correct angle on the page.

Figure 3.8 Pencil-sighting is an effective technique for determining angles, especially angles of perspective. (Campo Santo; Pisa, IT [top]. Unity Temple; Oak Park, IL [bottom].)

◆ **Pencil-Sighting (Method 2):** The second method for using pencil-sighting allows for reasonably precise measurements of proportion, which is the relative dimension of one object to another. This method is not based on systematic units of length, such as inches or centimeters. It is only intended to give a rough guide as to estimated units, created on-site, by using the pencil as a ruler. While keeping one eye closed, hold the pencil between the object being measured and your open eye, and mark the object's length from the end of the pencil with your thumb. Then use this measurement to determine the relative length of other objects in the view. It is critically important that you keep the pencil a very consistent distance from your eye, or the measurements will be inaccurate. Some people always hold the pencil at full arm's length to maintain this consistency. I prefer to flex my elbow, but I am always careful to keep the same distance between my eye and the pencil when making a set of quick measurements.

Figure 3.9   Pencil-sighting is also effective for measuring relative proportions. First measure an object in the view, then use this measurement to determine the relative sizes of other objects. (Hawthorne District; Portland, OR.)

Choosing Subjects

In selecting potential subjects for a sketch, several issues should be considered. First, at the most general level, think about what interests you. Is it architecture, or public spaces, or a combination of the two? Are you more interested in smaller elements such as doorways or windows? Is it the sense of urban life that you would like to capture, which would entail a focus on people and activity? Or are you most interested in trees and other landscape elements? In trying to draw what you see around you, it is most common that several of these elements will combine to create a complete sketch, but your particular interest should be the first guide in determining what subjects you select.

Figure 3.10   The same subject, and resulting sketches, at two times during the same day—in sun (top) and shade (bottom). (Art & Architecture South Building, University of Idaho; Moscow, ID.)

Light is a critical aspect of most representational sketches. Look for situations where the contrast is clear between areas of sunlight and areas of shade, and select a vantage point from which this contrast is most evident. If a particular subject looks appealing, but lacks an interesting combination of light and shade, try to figure out what time of day would be best and return to do the sketch at that time. Avoid sketching subjects that are entirely in shadow. It will be very difficult to depict spatial volumes without light and shade, and it is also difficult to see any detail or material when surfaces are shaded. Another problem with drawing heavily shaded subjects is that you will spend a lot of time laying down areas of value on the page, and the result is often a dark sketch with little sense of clarity or focus. Finally, a good reason for avoiding these lighting situations is to protect your eyes—they will tire quickly if you have to look toward the direct sun while sketching.

It's a common mistake to find a comfortable place to sit and only then begin to look around for an interesting subject. This is certainly one way of finding subjects to sketch, but I strongly recommend that the subject be identified first. Spend some time walking around, all the while looking for appropriate sketching subjects. If you are in an urban space, such as a piazza or plaza, walk around the perimeter and through the center. If you are on a street, walk up and down some of its length. Observe the light and shade, architectural compositions, human activity, materials and details, etc., before settling on an interesting subject. Think carefully about the most effective point of view. For example, move closer to the subject for a more dramatic perspective, or further away to include more of the surrounding context. Move left or right to see how the light and perspective change.

If there is a convenient place to sit, that allows you to see your subject from the desired point of view, then have a seat and begin sketching. But if there is no convenient place to sit, don't sacrifice an interesting point of view for comfort. Sketching on your feet has at least a few benefits. First, it's more likely that the perspective will be convincing, and give a better sense of what the space is like from the point of view of someone moving through the city on foot. Second, your body will be more active in making the sketch, as you shift your weight from one foot to the other, which often results in a more energetic sketch. Third, you'll have a better chance of not overworking the sketch, or getting too deeply involved in detail. You'll be much more likely to keep things brief and direct, and thus more likely to create a lively sketch rather than a laborious drawing. Sketching while standing can be a challenge—it can be tiring and it can be difficult to juggle your sketching gear, especially if you are working with watercolors. To deal with these challenges, sometimes the best strategy is to do most, if not all, of the sketch setup while standing, and then find a place very nearby to sit and add value and/or color.

There are times of the year when outdoor sketching is not possible, and even in the summer months there will be days of rain. Sketching indoors may not offer the same variety of street scenes and the wonderful contrast created by strong, clear sunlight. But don't let this stop you—coffee shops, indoor shopping centers, places of worship, and museums are excellent places to practice sketching. Art museums, in particular, provide an endless source of worthwhile sketching subjects, whether you sketch sculpture, paintings, or the gallery spaces.

Figure 3.11   Sketch completed of a favorite painting that was on loan to an accessible art museum, during a day of inclement weather. "Supper at Emmaus" by Caravaggio
The Art Institute of Chicago (temporary exhibit)
Chicago, IL
October 23, 2009
Copic Multiliner SP (Black)
Small Moleskine Sketchbook

Planning and Beginning the Sketch

The specific steps involved in sketching are covered thoroughly in subsequent chapters, but a few words about these steps are worth mentioning here, as is some general advice about the process of sketching. I most often think of constructing a sketch in two steps: setup and value. All the other aspects of a sketch can be considered under these two general headings. The two steps can overlap somewhat in practice, but their order is important. Setup must come first, and it may be enough for a complete sketch by itself. Value adds the characteristic of light, and, potentially, texture and detail. Both steps together will constitute a complete sketch, which is typically the case with graphite sketches and most ink sketches. Color is treated separately in this book, because color may be added to a sketch that has been set up properly and given value, or color may take the place of value. In some cases, color alone may be used to complete both steps at once, without a preliminary sketch in graphite or ink, but the essential steps of setup and value must be considered even if you are working only in color.

Figure 3.12 Before beginning, consider what will be the focus and what will be the extents of the sketch. In this example, the darkest region would be left out, the light-gray region would be included as context, and the main focus would be on the colorful buildings at the center of the composition. (Via del Tempio; Rome, IT.)

It is best to develop the various elements of a sketch in some sort of order, taking one subject at a time, working from the large-scale aspects of the sketch to the small scale, and beginning with overall layout before finishing with value. But all these elements should be considered as a whole as you begin—think of this as "planning" the sketch. For example, the chapter titled "Entourage" treats some elements of drawing as a separate topic, and the implication is that these elements should be added toward the end of the sketch. But entourage elements should always be considered and anticipated, if not actually drawn, during the setup of a sketch. If you don't make some light marks or lines to indicate where these elements will go, you may end up with a beautifully sketched street scene with no room for people, cars, café umbrellas, trees, etc.

Whether you tend to rely more on composition or perspective (discussed in Chapter 4: Setup), or a balance of the two, it is helpful to visualize the sketch on the page before you make any marks. The sight-sizing method described above is an excellent way to do this. Begin by determining the focus of the sketch—what is the most interesting aspect of your view? Perhaps it is a particular building, doorway, or outdoor café. Then consider how much of the surrounding context will be required to describe the immediate environment around your focus. How much of the street or plaza will need to be included? How much of the sky should be shown? How much of the view to the left or right of your focus will help tell the story of what you see? Once you have a good understanding of what will be included, and what will be excluded, visualize this information on the page. Start with the tallest vertical and the widest horizontal dimension of the sketch, and arrange these on the page so that the entire drawing will fit as desired. It's good practice to account for a half-inch or more of white space to surround the area intended for the sketch, and to block out any areas intended for text.

The first marks you make on the page are certainly very important, but they don't need to be "correct" in a strict sense. Instead, they should be used simply to arrange the major elements of the drawing. It's important to be patient during this phase of the sketch, to be sure that the overall composition is correct before moving on to value. Strive to be as accurate as possible, without being overly concerned with precision. Don't worry if you draw a line that's not quite right, and don't erase. Simply redraw the line in its correct position, even if it requires two or three attempts to get it right. Erasing gets in the way of forward progress, and it actually prevents you from learning from your mistakes. Also, erasing can mar the surface of the paper, which is especially problematic when working with watercolor, leading to splotchy washes on the page. If the first marks on the page are kept very light and thin, any mistakes will eventually be obscured by additional sketching.

The instructions in this and the following chapter are intended to help you develop a way of seeing, and translating what you see onto a two-dimensional page. What you see and what your brain processes are not always the same thing, and it is important to be able to separate these perceptions to sketch what you see with any accuracy. In the very short time between observation and sketching—when the eyes go from looking at a subject to looking at the sketch—a lot can happen to distort what was observed. The brain will attempt to process the purely visual information into something it deems more useful, or often into something more familiar but less visually accurate. The instructions presented here will help you transfer what you see to the page. The more you apply these techniques, the more you will learn to trust your eyes. Sight-sizing is an effective strategy on its own, but it becomes even more powerful when combined with other skills of observation, especially composition and perspective.

CHAPTER

4 *SETUP*

The first steps taken in constructing a sketch are extremely important. If one or more of the major guidelines are significantly out of place, subsequent elements will not fit or they will be out of proportion. If a sketch is begun in this way—poorly composed, or with inaccurate guidelines—there is nothing that can be added to improve it. Yet it is common for beginners to avoid the process of laying out the entire sketch, or to go through it too quickly and thus not thoroughly enough. Often, we would like to see what the finished sketch will look like, so we focus on sketching the value and details too soon in the process. There is also a tendency to start a sketch on one element in the view and work outward from there, or to begin in the upper-left corner of the page, and work our way down and to the right, as if writing text. These impulses should be suppressed in favor of working out the structure, or the "setup" of the entire drawing first. Some have referred to this as *building* a sketch, and I think the analogy is apt—think of the setup as the foundation for a well-constructed sketch.

The most effective strategy for building an accurate sketch, and the one that seems to be overlooked most frequently, is to lay out the entire sketch in light lines first, getting the overall proportions of height, width, and angles into their correct position. This requires patience in seeking out the structure of the sketch and establishing an interesting, compelling, and, above all, accurate composition. This step cannot be overemphasized, and it cannot be practiced too much. It needs to become a habit that value and detail are not added until the entire sketch is effectively mapped out. Practice repeatedly until this step becomes relatively easy to accomplish. Setting up the sketch can be more difficult with pen and ink, even if you are using a very fine-lined pen. When using ink, try placing dots on the page instead of lines, as shown in Figure 3.4 (drawing straight lines). When you are reasonably certain of their proper location, connect the appropriate dots to complete the setup. With graphite, it is quite easy to sketch very light lines—use a well-sharpened, relatively hard pencil, such as an HB, H, or 2H.

Setting up a sketch can be accomplished in several ways, but there are two general approaches that can be equally effective—composition and perspective. Each can be employed independently, or they can be blended as necessary or in whatever way is most useful for a given situation. The principles of composition presented here will suffice in setting up a sketch, and they are relatively simple to comprehend and apply, so these should be mastered first. But it helps to have a grasp of basic perspective as well. I've found that combining elements of both approaches is the most effective strategy—freely using compositional techniques in conjunction with perspective will lead to sketches that are set up as well as possible. Regardless of the strategies you acquire and develop in your own work, always be patient and do not move too quickly through this stage of a sketch. Also, if you are working in a sketchbook and plan to add text, be sure to reserve space on the page for this purpose.

Figure 4.1 An example of a sketch that has been set up thoroughly (top) before the addition of value, and the resulting final sketch (below right).
Castel Sant'Angelo
Rome, IT
July 16, 2011
HB and 2B Pencils

Figure 4.2   Example of an incomplete sketch, showing the setup lines and partial shading. In the process of adding value across the entire sketch, some additional setup lines would be lightly sketched in. This was a very quick sketch—just 15 minutes—so the attention to detail is minimal and the shading is quite loose.
Fontana di Trevi
Rome, IT
July 2, 2010
2B Pencil

Composition

Composition is a strategy for placing the essential elements of a sketch properly on the page, using simple geometric positioning. Major elements of the view are located with respect to their relative size, shape, or angle, as if putting a puzzle together piece by piece. Composition allows you to transfer what you see to the page without needing to know anything about the rules of perspective. To effectively use composition as an independent strategy for setting up a sketch, it is most helpful to begin by using a viewfinder, as discussed in the previous chapter. Eventually, you should find less need for this device, and it is best not to develop too strong a reliance on it—after learning the effective use of a viewfinder, try working without one as described later in this section.

Using the example from Chapter 3 (Figure 3.11), we can graphically describe the essential steps for composing a sketch. First, draw a rectangle, or "frame," on the page, matching the same proportions of the viewfinder. The frame does not need to have the same dimensions as the viewfinder window, but the relative width to height must be the same. The entire page may be used as the frame, but the proportions of the page would need to match those of the viewfinder's opening. So if the viewfinder's window is 2 units wide by 3 units tall, the rectangle drawn on the page must also be 2 units by 3 units. The viewfinder's window might be 6" × 4", for example. The frame on the page should have the same proportions, if not the same size—so 3" × 2" would work. After the frame has been sketched, lightly draw grid lines, dividing the frame into quadrants as shown in Figure 4.3b. Remember to hold the viewfinder a consistent distance from your eye when observing the sketch subject, and begin to look for major lines in the view that correspond to the grid. For example, the long vertical edge of the pale yellow building on the right aligns with the grid line ¼ distance from the right of the frame, and the vertical edge of the dark building to the left is approximately midway between the left boundary of the viewfinder, and the grid line ¼ distance from this boundary. Looking at the building just left of center, the ridge of the roof is just below the grid line, ¼ distance from the top of the frame. Continue making observations through the viewfinder, finding major elements of the view—prominent vertical and horizontal lines—and transferring these elements to the sketch, using the frame and grid lines as guides. Be sure to work your way around the entire sketch at this early stage, rather than focusing too long on any particular area.

Figure 4.3a Observing a sketch subject through a viewfinder, as described in Chapter 3, and envisioning grid lines dividing the view into vertical and horizontal quadrants. (Via del Tempio; Rome, Italy.)

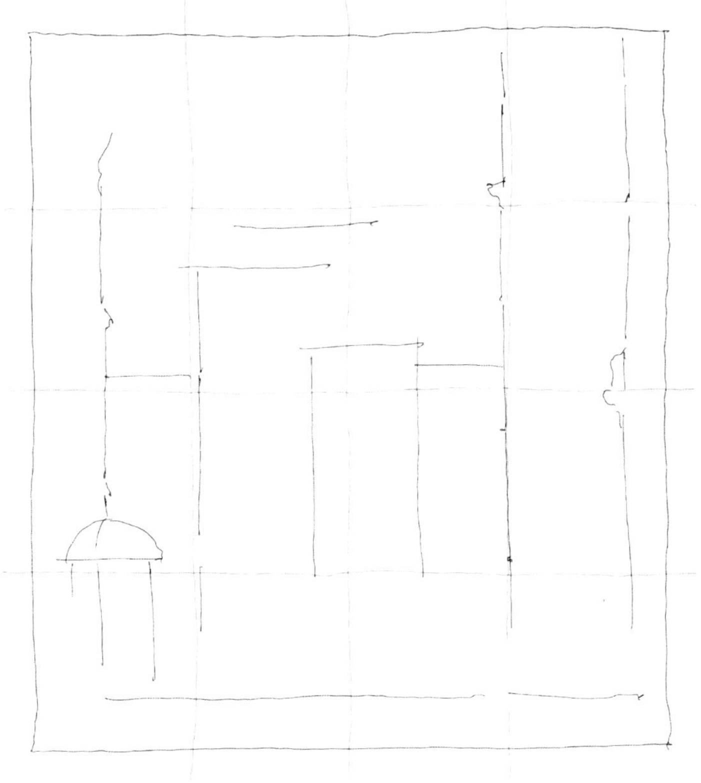

Figure 4.3b   A sketched frame and grid lines, of the same proportions as the viewfinder, with several of the major vertical and horizontal elements of the view positioned with respect to the frame and grid.

Figure 4.3c   The sketch more or less fully composed, with the necessary elements in place. Notice the additional grids used to align the windows with one another.

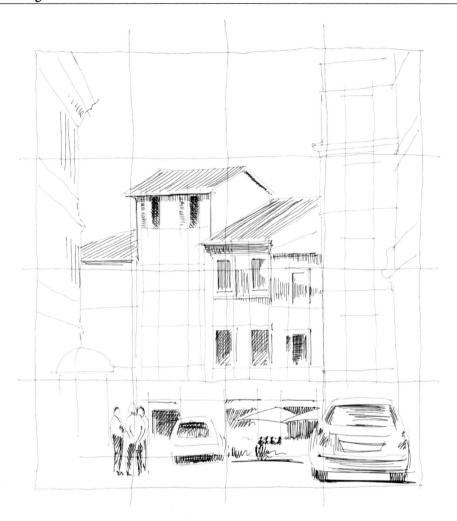

Figure 4.3d   Adding value to the composed sketch with simple hatch patterns. Notice the direction of the hatch on the roofs, and the cross-hatch patterns for added darkness in the windows.

When most of the major elements have been sketched in, you can begin to use these lines (in addition to the grid lines and frame) as your guide. Try to estimate the angles of cornice lines, as seen on the buildings to the left and right, and begin to lay out guidelines for repeated rectilinear elements such as the windows (Figure 4.3c). At this stage, it is also a good idea to rough-in some entourage elements such as people and vehicles. Once the majority of the sketch has been "set up" in this way, it will be clear   value and texture—Figure 4.2d shows this partially completed.

In the next example (Figure 4.4), the major horizontal lines   gn with the ½ and ¼ horizontal grid lines. This is by virtue of the way the photograph wa   , which can be the same when you use a viewfinder—think of it as composing a photo using a   s viewfinder, or what is seen on the screen of a digital camera. Establish "landmarks" in the view, so   each time you need to look through the viewfinder, it is easy to recapture the view you are working on a precisely as possible. In this image, it would be easy to reestablish the view by aligning the ground line (where the building meets the ground) with the horizontal midpoint line of the viewfinder, and the roof line and the reflection of the roof line with the ¼ horizontal lines.

Figure 4.4a A horizontal composition, involving the reflection of a simple building form in water. (Chapel of St. Ignatius; Seattle, WA.)

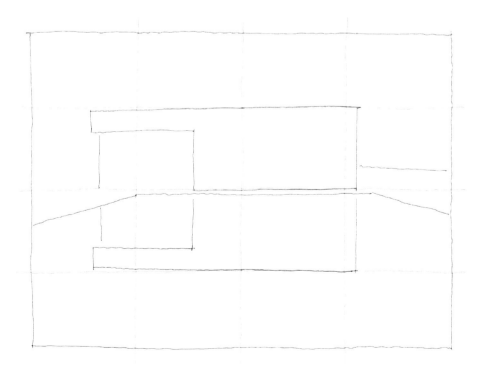

Figure 4.4b The major horizontal and vertical lines, positioned with respect to a grid.

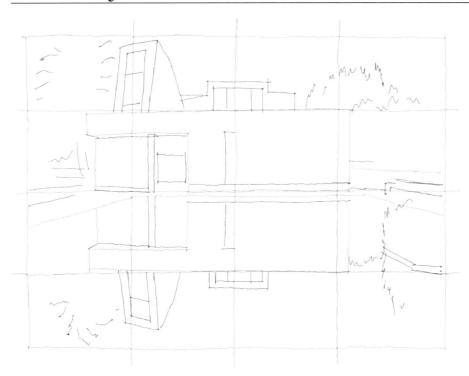

Figure 4.4c Additional shapes positioned with respect to the grid and the major horizontals and verticals in the view.

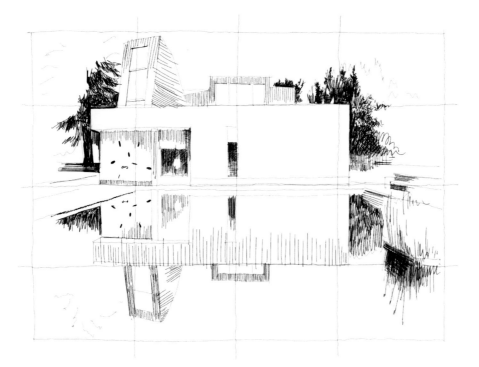

Figure 4.4d Adding value. Notice the random—but not "sloppy"—patterns used to develop the landscape elements such as trees and shrubs, providing a dark contrast against the light surfaces of the building.

Notice that the roof line and its reflection are not perfectly horizontal. Toward the left of the view, they bow toward each other slightly. This is the result of the increasing distance between the viewer and the roof lines, and is an issue that will be covered later in this chapter, in the section on perspective. For now, be observant of subtle (and perhaps unexpected) situations such as this. These "horizontal" lines might be expected to be truly horizontal for their entire length, but careful observation proves otherwise. Remember to use pencil-sighting (Figure 3.8) to check your initial assumptions. You may begin to find that straight lines—roof lines, ground lines, etc.—will often appear to curve, based on their changing distance from the observer. Since one of the goals of representational sketching is to create a reasonably accurate visual depiction of the subject, this type of observation deserves careful attention.

Often, the subject is not as simple as in the previous example, and the major lines are neither horizontal nor vertical, but are instead a variety of angles. In these cases, the angles may be estimated according to their position relative to the viewfinder and to one another. In Figure 4.5, there are two major verticals that coincide, more or less, with the ¼ grid marks on the viewfinder. The ochre-colored building to the left meets the roof of the central building at precisely the ¼ mark, while the white building on the right ends just inside the ¼ mark. It would make sense to begin by sketching these two lines first, as almost every other line in this view is angled to some degree (and even these two lines are not truly vertical—they angle slightly inward toward the top, again because they get farther away from the viewer as they rise).

The next line we might try to sketch could be "Line I" in Figure 4.5b, because its starting point at upper right is easy to identify, being very close to the upper-right corner of the viewfinder (A). We also notice that

Figure 4.5a   A complex subject, involving various angles. (Piazza del Biscione; Rome, IT.)

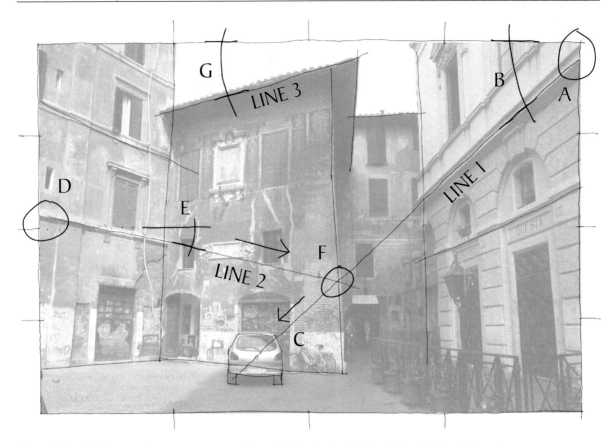

Figure 4.5b   Graphic notes for positioning some of the major lines in the view. See the text for descriptions of noted elements.

the angle of this line is approximately 45° from the top boundary of the frame (B). It often helps to extend some lines in the sketch and to look for places where they would intersect with other lines or objects in the view. This line, if carried beyond the edge of the white building to the right, intersects with the center of the car (C), just about at the ground line of the central building. Rather than continuing to focus on the lines of the white building on the right, look for other lines that will help to organize the entire sketch. The next line we might work on could be "Line 2" in Figure 4.5b, as it begins just above the center point along the left edge of the viewfinder. Its angle (E) is more difficult to estimate than that of Line 1, so pencil-sighting may be helpful here. When Line 2 is extended to intersect Line 1, they meet at the right edge of the central building, which is just to the right of the vertical center line of the frame (F). Line 3 is perhaps the most important line yet to be positioned, and this line is more challenging than the others mentioned so far. It is not anchored to an obvious position on the viewfinder, such as a corner or midpoint, and its angle (G) is again difficult to estimate without the use of pencil-sighting. But by using the viewfinder, and by working within the frame and the lines that have already been drawn (the major verticals and Lines 1 and 2), it will be much easier to establish the proper location and angle of Line 3.

After working around the entire view, most of the major lines of the sketch will be established, as seen in Figure 4.5c. These provide guidelines for further delineation of the sketch. At this point, while the setup is well underway, it is not yet complete—the locations of doors, windows, and other small-scale elements have yet to be identified. Be careful not to skip ahead to value at this stage of the sketch. Push the setup further until there are guidelines for the smaller elements, as seen in Figure 4.5d.

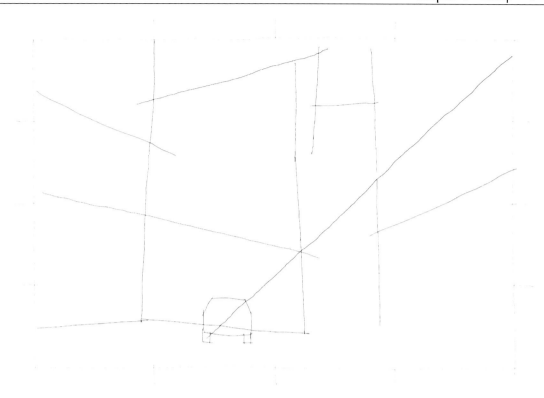

Figure 4.5c   With the locations and angles of the major lines established, the setup is partially complete.

Figure 4.5d   A completed setup, with virtually all the necessary guidelines sketched lightly into place.

Figure 4.5e Value and detail being added to the sketch.

In Figure 4.5e, some of the value has been added. Notice how some areas are hatched quite heavily, and others lightly, but in all cases, the direction of the hatch patterns has been carefully considered. In some places, the "hatch" pattern is actually used to indicate the presence of window shutters, or reflections on glass, or the exposed bricks at bottom center. In other cases, the marks are used to describe details, such as the sculptural wall panels on the central building, or the graffiti and the bicycle. These techniques will be covered with greater attention in Chapter 5, Value, but for now, observe the subtle differences between what is considered "value" and what is considered "detail."

The three preceding examples relied on the use of a viewfinder and a sketched, rectangular frame on the page, but composition may also be used without these devices. The strategy still involves observing and recording the basic two-dimensional relationships of the elements within view. Using a frame might be thought of as working from the outside in, where the outer limits of the frame provide the starting point for the sketch. By not using a frame, one needs to work from the inside out, perhaps beginning with a prominent vertical or horizontal line or edge in the view.

Begin by identifying the greatest vertical and horizontal dimensions of the sketch subject. The tower is the tallest vertical element, and the width from the right edge of the tower to the left edge of the central building is the overall width. Since the sketch will include some surrounding context, be sure to provide some additional space around the perimeter as you arrange the drawing on the page. The context in this case would include portions of the buildings to left and right of the central subject, the cars and landscape in the foreground, and white space at the top to indicate the sky. It's always a good idea to overestimate the space needed for

Figure 4.6a   Finding the overall dimensions of the sketch—the vertical and horizontal of greatest length. The edge of the image has been blurred to emphasize that, in this case, we are not working within a predefined frame. (Chicago Theological Seminary; Chicago, IL.)

surrounding context—better to have too much blank space around the sketch than to run out of room on the page. Taking these factors into consideration, place two lines on the page as shown in Figure 4.6b. The prominent tower in this view might suggest a vertical orientation on the page, but since there will be some context to the left and right, the overall horizontal dimension will be greater than the vertical. If the tower was the primary focus of the sketch, I would more likely orient the sketch vertically on the page, leaving out more of the building to the left. But if the composition is to include both the tower and its associated building—as well as some context—a horizontal orientation makes more sense. After a fair amount of practice, you should be able to quickly assess the sketch subject and place its greatest dimensions on the page. Sight-sizing (Figure 3.7) is an excellent technique for accelerating this process.

Once it is clear how the major vertical and horizontal dimensions will sit on the page, the subsequent elements may be developed from these lines. In Figure 4.6c, the first vertical line from Figure 4.6b has been used as the central corner of the tower, and two additional lines have been drawn to represent the tower's outer edges. A few short lines have been placed at the top of the tower to mark horizontal points—one where the tower narrows, for example, and another at the very top. A longer horizontal is drawn about halfway up the tower, indicating the common height of the roof peak of the left building and the roof eave of the right building. This is simply a guideline—it doesn't appear in the view, but it is helpful to draw during the setup. Even if lines like this remain in the finished sketch, they rarely detract from the image, so you should make as many dots and guidelines as you feel are necessary. Do not worry about littering the page with extraneous marks—it's far more important that the sketch is set up effectively, and after value is added to the sketch, these marks will become less prominent.

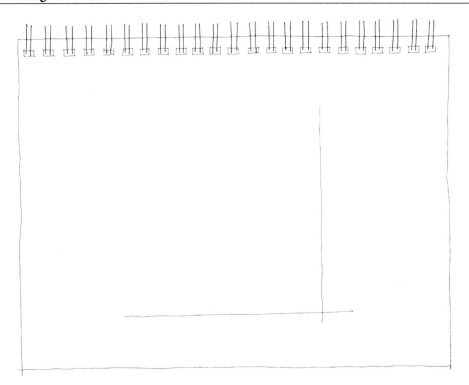

Figure 4.6b   Placing lines to represent the greatest vertical and horizontal on the page.

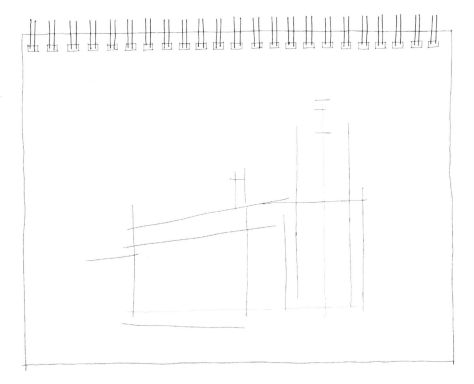

Figure 4.6c   Building the sketch from the basis of the greatest vertical and horizontal dimensions.

The most important setup lines, in addition to those outlining the tower, are the roof lines of the building on the left. These may appear to be horizontal, but in fact they slope down slightly to the left. Once again, pencil-sighting can help determine their approximate angles and their lengths (see Figures 3.8 and 3.9). Once enough additional elements have been added to the setup, value may be added to complete the sketch.

Composition is a set of strategies for being able to see relationships among elements in a view—among the buildings, people, vehicles, trees, etc. It requires that we assume the view is already two-dimensional, and using a viewfinder will help to reinforce this idea in practice. But the world is three-dimensional, and things appear the way they do for some simple reasons. This is where an understanding of perspective would greatly augment and be integrated with composition in setting up a sketch.

Figure 4.6d   Adding more elements to the sketch, working from the existing lines.

Figure 4.6e   Adding some value to give the sketch form and depth.

Perspective

Perspective is a fascinating topic, though it can be difficult to teach and learn if a thorough understanding is desired. There are many good books available on the subject, but most are directed toward designers who must be able to generate perspective drawings of imagined places (known as *constructed perspectives*), rather than sketch existing places from observation. When constructing perspectives from the imagination, far more must be understood regarding rules and techniques. There are a variety of approaches advocated by various teachers and authors, though even the most straightforward strategies require much time and practice to employ effectively. Most books on perspective attempt to cover virtually every possible situation, making the subject appear complex and confusing. One reason for such thorough instruction is the need for precision—it's important to be precise when crafting a perspective from scratch, and accurate measurements are needed to represent imagined spaces. Learning all the various rules and procedures for constructing perspectives can be daunting for someone who would simply like to sketch from observation. Paul Laseau, in his excellent book *Freehand Sketching*, goes so far as to state that, "while perspective is a handy device to construct imagined spaces, it is not useful, and possibly detrimental, to sketching existing environments." (p 32–33) Perspective can be a confusing subject, but I don't entirely agree with this assessment. While too much focus on perspective can lead to unnecessary confusion while sketching on location, understanding some of the basics can be extremely helpful, especially when combined with compositional techniques. So a thorough knowledge of perspective and a high degree of precision are unnecessary when sketching from observation. For these reasons, I have tried to keep the topic as simple as possible in this book. In practice, trying to apply perspective techniques too rigorously can make the process of sketching overly tedious, but some essential strategies can lead to easier and more successful drawing experiences.

Diminution

The first and most important general idea regarding perspective is that objects appear to diminish in size as their distance from the observer increases. This visual phenomenon, known as *diminution*, is the basis for the rules of perspective that are of greatest use in sketching from observation. A simple graphic that illustrates diminution is seen in Figure 4.7. If you were standing in the position of the person in this sketch, the near end of the wall on your right would appear to be taller than the far end of the wall, and the nearest tree on your left would appear to be taller than the tree in the distance at the far end of the row. The space between each pair of trees also appears to diminish as the distance from the viewer increases.

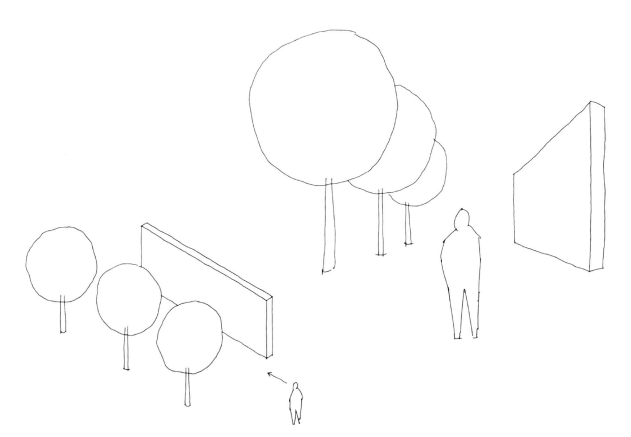

Figure 4.7   "Diminution" is the visual phenomenon of objects appearing to decrease in size as their distance from the observer increases.

Convergence and Vanishing Points

If the wall or the line of trees were to continue, they would appear to "vanish" at some point very far in the distance—this is called a *vanishing point*. Groups of lines that are parallel to one another in space will appear to converge on the same vanishing point, a visual phenomenon known as *convergence*. In Figure 4.8, the lines or rows of objects that are parallel to one another, such as the top and bottom of the wall and the implied line where the trees meet the ground, will converge on a single vanishing point. Looked at in another way, these lines appear to radiate from the same vanishing point.

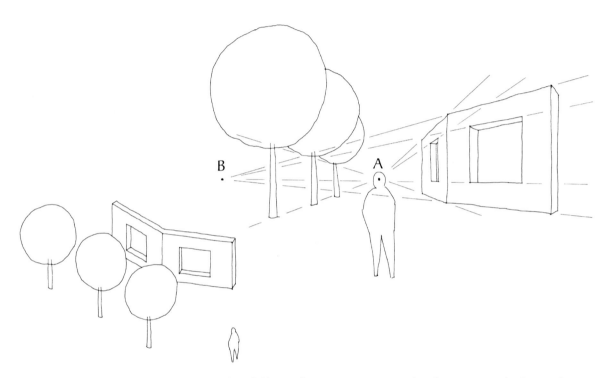

Figure 4.8 "Convergence" means that groups of parallel lines will appear to meet at or radiate from a point in the distance, known as a *vanishing point*. The point at "A" is the vanishing point for the horizontal lines of the row of trees on the left, and of the wall parallel to the trees on the right. The point at "B" is the vanishing point for the horizontal lines of the angled wall at far right.

Eye Level and Horizon Line

The next important perspective concept relates to the viewer's position with respect to their environment. Specifically, the height of the viewer's eyes, or one's "eye level," affects how objects will appear from their point of view. Think of the eye level as an invisible, horizontal plane that intersects the viewer's eyes and extends outward to infinity (Figure 4.9). One's eye level is not an object fixed in space; it is something that each individual carries with them, wherever they go. If we imagine seeing this plane at its farthest distance, it becomes what is called the *horizon line*. This is what we see when we stand on an ocean beach and look out to sea on a clear, calm day; it's the line where the ocean meets the sky. In most situations, the horizon line is not so clearly visible, yet it is always there as an imaginary line at the viewer's eye level. So the two terms, eye level and horizon line, are almost synonymous—they are not precisely the same thing, but they are directly related to one another, and in practice the terms are effectively interchangeable. In sketching, it can help to draw the horizon line on the page, and to build the sketch from this line.

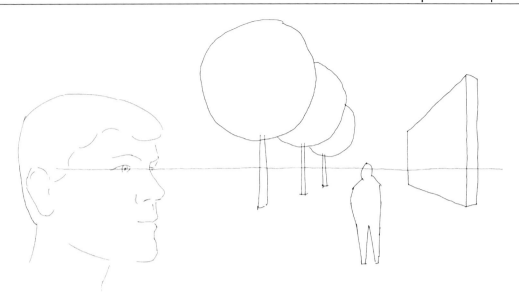

Figure 4.9   The viewer's eye level is an imaginary horizontal plane or line at the level of one's eyes. If we draw a line at this level on the sketch, it is called the *horizon line*.

Finding the Horizon Line

Since the horizon line is not always easily visible in a given view, it helps to have some strategies for locating it. Using the phenomenon of convergence is the most common method. By observing the points at which horizontal lines converge (vanishing points), a good approximation can be made to locate the horizon line. Start by finding at least one vanishing point as determined by a group of parallel horizontal lines. If you are able to locate more than one of these points, so much the better to find the horizon line. Buildings that are constructed of materials with obvious horizontal seams can be very helpful, such as those made of brick or horizontal siding. Try to see

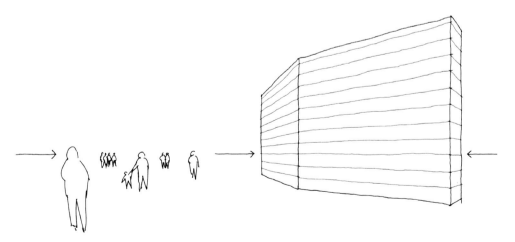

Figure 4.10   To find the horizon line, look for horizontal materials or other lines on nearby buildings. The horizon line is where the lines of materials are truly horizontal, rather than being angled up or down (at the arrows adjacent to the wall on the right). On flat surfaces, the horizon line will be where the heads of most people of average height line up.

where the seams appear to be flat rather than angled—this will locate the horizon line (Figure 4.10). You might also look to where people in the distance are at your eye level—their heads will help determine the height of the horizon line. A common problem in setting up sketches is placing the eye level too high. The result is a sketch that appears to have been drawn by a very tall person, or someone who is looking out of a second- or third-story window. So be sure to establish the eye level, or horizon line, very carefully as you begin the setup.

Horizontal and Sloping Lines

Lines that are horizontal in space (i.e., parallel to the flat ground) will converge on vanishing points that are on the horizon line. Lines that are parallel to one another but not horizontal will converge on vanishing points somewhere above or below the horizon line, depending on their angle and the position of the viewer. If the slope formed by parallel angled lines rises away from the viewer, like the ramp on the right in Figure 4.11, the vanishing point for these lines will be above the horizon line. If the slope falls away from the viewer, like the roof on the left, the vanishing point will be below the horizon line. If the sloping line is on a rectilinear grid in plan, its vanishing point will be directly above or below the vanishing point for horizontal lines on the same grid.

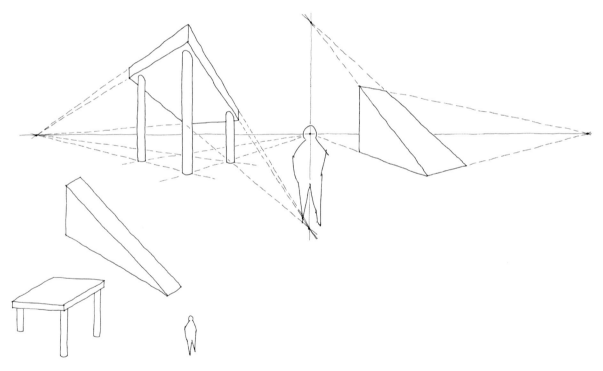

Figure 4.11 Sets of parallel lines that are not horizontal, such as a ramp or a sloping roof, will converge on or radiate from vanishing points above or below the horizon line.

Multiple Vanishing Points

In constructed perspectives, we commonly speak of "one-point," "two-point," or "three-point," referring to the number of vanishing points used to set up the drawing. But for sketching on location these terms are of limited use, because there may be any number of vanishing points in a particular view. In a situation such as the typical US city, which is organized on a grid, there will most often be one or two dominant vanishing points. But in urban places that are not organized this way—the randomly angled or curving streets in medieval European

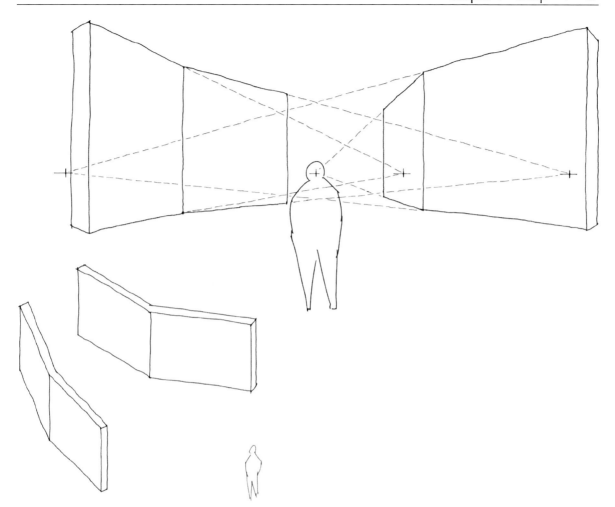

Figure 4.12   When there are numerous sets of parallel horizontal lines, there will be numerous vanishing points along the horizon line.

cities, for example—there are often many vanishing points. In these cases the vanishing points are as numerous as the groups of parallel lines that define the building façades, which are often oriented differently than their neighbors. Rather than thinking that every sketch will fall into the categories of "one-point" or "two-point" perspectives, it is more important to be able to identify the various locations of vanishing points that affect the sketch setup by carefully observing groups of parallel lines.

Vanishing Points Off the Page

The value of locating vanishing points is that, once they have been established, the points may be used to help determine the angles of additional lines. If we are able to locate a vanishing point by observing the roof and ground line of a building, for example, we can sketch additional lines from that point to align rows of windows or other building elements. When sketching a street scene, it is common for at least one of the vanishing points to be located somewhere in the composition, or at least somewhere on the page, making it easy to use the points in further developing the sketch. But there will be times when the vanishing point(s) will not be conveniently located on the page. In these instances, the location of the point may need to be visualized adjacent to the sketchbook.

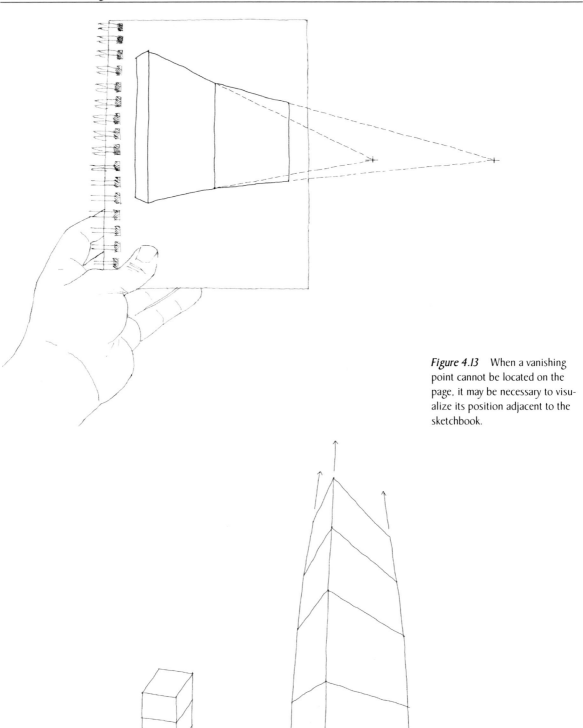

Figure 4.13   When a vanishing point cannot be located on the page, it may be necessary to visualize its position adjacent to the sketchbook.

Figure 4.14   Tall vertical lines will appear to converge on a vanishing point directly above the observer.

Vertical Vanishing Point

In most cases, the vertical lines in a view—the corners of buildings, for example—will appear to be straight up and down, and may be drawn this way. But when surrounding buildings or towers are quite tall, vertical lines in space (all of which are effectively parallel to one another) will appear to converge on a single point directly over the viewer's position. I refer to this as a *vertical vanishing point*. This is sometimes referred to as *three-point perspective*, though this is a misnomer, as it assumes there are never more than two vanishing points for horizontal lines. Since the vertical vanishing point is directly above the observer, its location must be estimated, but it is usually sufficient to assume that it is directly above the center of the sketch, far off the page.

Repeated Modules in Perspective

There are many cases where a view will include repeated modules—a row of columns or arches, a series of doors or windows, etc. In order to measure their diminishing size as they recede from the viewer, a simple technique may be used. Begin by establishing the vanishing point for the parallel horizontal lines, and use compositional strategies to determine the width of one module (Figure 4.15, top). Then draw a line from the vanishing point that intersects the center of the module in height (Line "A" in the middle sketch). By drawing a diagonal line from "B" through the intersection of Line A and the next vertical line of the module (at "C"), the location of the module's next vertical line can be determined ("D"). Repeat the process as necessary in either direction. This technique can be used for any modular element in a sketch. Windows are a good example—a common mistake is to draw each window individually, guessing at their relative sizes. It is far easier, and considerably faster, to draw very light guidelines that define the common sills, heads, and jambs of the windows, and to use the diagonal technique to regulate their size and spacing.

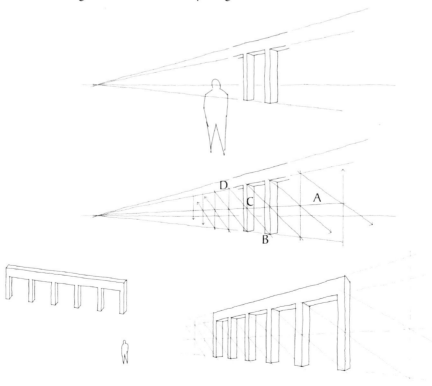

Figure 4.15   Using diagonal lines drawn through a center-height line, the spacing of repeated modules can be determined with reasonable accuracy.

Catedral de Barcelona, cloister. 7.5.09

Figure 4.16   An example of a sketch that relied on the repeated modules technique demonstrated in Figure 4.15.
Cathedral Cloister
Barcelona, SP
July 5, 2009
2B Pencil
25 minutes

Curves in Perspective

If you are faced with horizontal or vertical circles, they will appear to be ellipses in perspective—wider or narrower depending on your point of view. An ellipse is like a squashed circle, with one axis longer than the other. Figure 4.17 shows a series of discs floating in space in front of the observer. When a disc is seen on edge (at the viewer's eye level), it will appear as a flat line, the same length as the long axes of the ellipses above and below the viewer's eye level. As the discs rise higher above or lower below the eye level, their short axis length-ens, making the ellipse appear thicker, top to bottom, while it remains the same width, side to side. It can help to visualize the circles inscribed within squares to see how perspective affects their dimensions (the middle pair of sketches in Figure 4.17). If the circles were oriented vertically, the same visual phenomenon occurs, as shown in the bottom pair of sketches. The example in Figure 4.18 combines ellipses oriented horizontally in the curve of the wall and vertically in the curves of the arches. Notice how the arches may be constructed using whole ellipses, with a long vertical axis and a short horizontal axis.

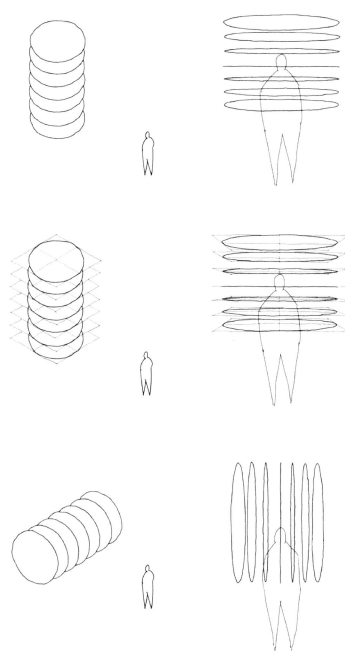

Figure 4.17   Circles, oriented horizontally and vertically, will appear as ellipses in perspective.

Figure 4.18   Using ellipses to sketch arches in a curving wall. (Colosseum; Rome, IT)

Curvilinear Perspective

Constructing perspectives from the imagination relies on what is called the *linear perspective*. It has the name *linear* because it requires that straight lines in space must be represented as being straight in the drawing as well. This underlying assumption forms the basis of linear perspective drawing—without it, constructing accurate perspectives from the imagination would be impossible. However, the way we actually see is quite different than the way it is replicated in linear perspective. The most important difference between linear perspective and the way we see is that straight lines in space are often perceived to be curved lines from particular points of view. The way we perceive space could rightly be called *curvilinear perspective*, and a basic understanding of this phenomenon can lead to sketches that more accurately represent our visual perception of the world. First, taking what we already know about perspective—that objects appear to diminish in size as their distance from the viewer increases—refer to Figure 4.19, which shows a long straight wall. The distance between the viewer and the wall is greater at the ends of the wall, so we would see the top and bottom lines of the wall moving toward one vanishing point to the left, and another to the right. But the lines cannot be drawn straight from each vanishing point, or the wall would appear to be somewhat diamond shaped (top). The correct way to indicate this situation, or to sketch it as our eyes see it, is to curve the top and the bottom lines of the wall—in effect, to join the left and right halves of the perspective smoothly.

This situation might seem relatively rare, but, when you begin to see it, you are likely to see it everywhere. Compared to a strict linear perspective, this is a more accurate representation of how we perceive space. In sketching on location, linear perspective is most useful when drawing subjects at a distance. But with curvilinear perspective, the viewer can inhabit the space through the drawing, because this approach allows us to draw something resembling peripheral vision.

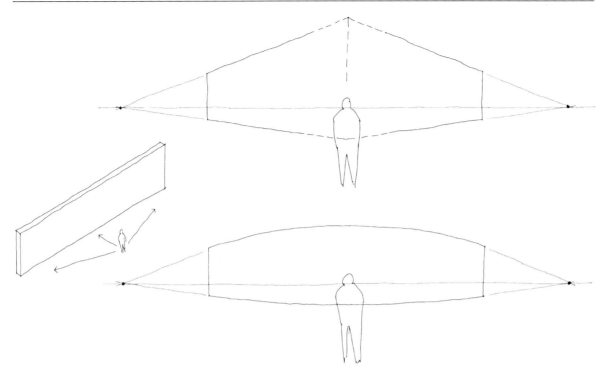

Figure 4.19   A simple diagram describing curvilinear perspective.

Figure 4.20   An example of the use of curvilinear perspective. Another example can be seen in the Trevi Fountain sketch in this chapter (Figure 4.2).
Train to Ostia Antica
Rome, IT
June 4, 2010
Uniball Vision Micro and Watercolor in Moleskine Large Watercolor Sketchbook (16" × 5")
30 minutes

Composition and perspective are intended to help you transfer what you see to the page. By using the techniques presented in this chapter, you should be able to set up a fairly accurate view in almost any situation. Practice these methods until you are able to apply them effectively, but avoid becoming too dependent on any particular technique. Strive for the ability to freely use composition and/or perspective as much—or as little—as is necessary to set up your sketches accurately. Regardless of your ability with these techniques, always remember to trust your eyes and draw what you see. Then move into applying value to the sketch to bring out the light and depth of your view.

CHAPTER

5 *VALUE*

Light is what allows our eyes to see, and the contrast between light and shade helps us to perceive the spaces we inhabit. If a sketch consists of nothing more than the outlines of buildings and other objects in view—that is, an unshaded line drawing—it will communicate a certain amount of information regarding shape, structure, and perhaps even depth, assuming the perspective has been set up successfully. But without the indication of light and shade, the sketch will be limited in its ability to convey form and depth of space. "Value" refers to the shaded tone of a sketch and its careful application will make the sketch a far more accurate representation of what we see. Once a sketch has been properly set up, the addition of value (whether monochromatic or full color) has the potential to bring the view to life. Strong value contrast attracts and excites our eyes. From the time our eyes first begin to develop, we are drawn to contrasts in light and color. Experiments have shown that infants are visually attracted to high-contrast imagery with bold colors and patterns, and sharp, clear edges. While we develop greater sensitivity to subtle contrast with age, strong contrast between light and dark continues to demand our attention, while muted tones generally fail to provoke much response. So value is a powerful tool in sketching. Beyond its ability to describe light and form, it can also create a sense of drama, catching the viewer's attention and drawing their eyes into the scene.

Not every sketch subject immediately lends itself to a rendering with strong value contrast. Look for situations and views where the contrasts are clear, and where the value distinctions will make for an interesting sketch. This sometimes means that a favorable subject will only be appropriate to sketch at a particular time of day, depending on sun angles. Refer to the comments made in relation to Figure 3.10, as a heavily shaded subject is often very difficult to draw in a way that describes its form clearly.

Since it is most common to sketch with dark media on light paper, what we are actually drawing is the absence of light, so we must learn to represent light by drawing darkness. This must be done selectively, however. There is often a tendency to apply value to an entire drawing. Almost everything we see in a view has at least some value—the exception might be a perfectly white wall in brilliant sunshine—so we might be inclined to apply at least some graphite or ink to every part of the sketch. This is almost always a mistake. Applying value to the entire sketch eliminates the possibility of using the white of the paper as the lightest value. With graphite or ink, if the whole sketch is some version of gray, the opportunity for a wide spectrum of tone is missed. Even when using watercolor, where very light-valued washes may be applied to the page, it is usually advisable to leave some amount of paper exposed as the very lightest value in a drawing. Another tendency is to be timid about the dark values, to not push them very far into the dark end of the value scale. This happens frequently when sketching in pencil, especially if the graphite is in the H range of hardness (see Figure 2.3), but also if the sketcher has a light touch.

Figure 5.1   A sketch with very bold value contrast, conveying a clear sense of light and a dramatic
impression of the canyon-like street.
Palazzo della Cancelleria
Rome, IT
July 19, 2011
HB Pencil on Fabriano Ruvido Drawing Paper (9" × 12")
45 minutes

Figure 5.2   A very quick sketch in charcoal, with lively hatching and bold values.
The Pantheon
Rome, IT
June 13, 2007
Medium Charcoal Pencil on Canson Drawing Paper (12" × 9")
20 minutes

To counteract these tendencies and develop skills for applying strong value, it helps to simplify the "value scheme," at least in the early stages of practice. A value scheme is simply the range of values in a given drawing. In simplifying the scheme, we reduce the total number of distinct values. So, rather than having ten or twelve different levels of tone on the page, we reduce this number significantly. Perhaps there are only three or four distinct values—the white of the paper is always the very lightest value, and there might be only two or three tonal values besides white, with one value that is very dark and two others that are intermediate. Simplifying the value scheme is a good way to condense the sketching process, to avoid getting bogged down in detail, and to produce images that are bold and clear. In terms of media, a charcoal pencil works well because, with a moderate amount of pressure, very dark black tones can be easily applied. But simplifying the value scheme is a worthwhile strategy no matter which drawing medium is used.

An excellent exercise for practicing value, and especially for simplifying the value scheme, is to do small, very brief studies of large-scale shadows, such as may be encountered in a typical street scene on a sunny day. When you are forced to keep a sketch very small and you have little time to draw, you'll be required to simplify the values and to be bold and dramatic in their application. This is very good practice, not only as you begin to sketch but as ongoing, periodic training for working with strong values. The sketches in Figure 5.3 (and Figure 1.10) were completed as a demonstration of this exercise at workshops in Lisbon, Portugal. Each sketch is approximately 2" wide by 3" tall, and each was done in about three minutes. With these parameters, I had no choice but to work quickly and boldly, ignoring the wealth of visible detail and color in the view before me and greatly simplifying the values. In these cases, I was using an earth-toned colored pencil, but a soft graphite or charcoal pencil would have been as effective. Again, in order to show light, we need to draw darkness—to show very bright light, we accentuate the darks and leave the white of the page untouched if a surface is in direct sunlight.

In addition to making a compelling sketch, value should be used to accentuate the primary focus. As discussed in relation to Figure 3.12, every sketch should have some sense of focus, formed around the most interesting aspect of the view you would like to capture. This is an essential aspect of framing and setting up a sketch

Figure 5.3 Quick value studies of a street in Lisbon, done as a demonstration in a workshop focused on light. Figure 1.10 shows similar studies from an earlier session of the same workshop.
Sunlight Studies, Rua das Portas
Lisbon, PT
July 23, 2011
Venetian Red on Fabriano Ruvido
Drawing Paper (9" × 12")
3 minutes each

and it comes to fruition in the way value is applied. The best general approach is to increase the value contrast in the focus area and decrease it in the surrounding context. The focus area should be given the lightest and darkest values of the sketch, in direct proximity to each other, and the level of precision should be increased in this area as well. So the darks should be sketched most boldly and most carefully where the focus is intended to be. The rest of the sketch may be handled more loosely—though never carelessly—and the relative values may be less dramatically contrasted. This approach will attract the viewer's eye toward the primary subject of the sketch while still providing the necessary context of the scene. In the case of Figure 5.4, the focus is on the roof eaves that come together at the center of the image, and on the darkly shaded figures at street level. As another example, the focus in Figure 5.1 is generally on the facade at right, but more specifically on the strong shadow on this facade. These elements have been drawn more carefully and with much more contrast than the buildings on the left, which are drawn with relatively little contrast.

Figure 5.4   Using strong value contrast to create a focus. Look for a similar effect in other examples throughout the book.
Via delle Vacche
Rome, IT
June 8, 2010
Watercolor on Arches Cold Press
(9" × 12")
45 minutes

Applying Value

The way that value is applied to a sketch will depend on the medium. Ink pens are limited to relatively thin lines, so the only way to generate areas of tone is to hatch and cross-hatch. With graphite, lines may again be used for hatching and cross-hatching, although with greater variety of width than ink pens allow. Also, the broad side of the pencil point, or a specially shaped point (see Figure 2.4), may be used for very wide strokes that will cover the page as a unified tone more quickly and evenly than hatched lines. This is one of the main reasons graphite pencils are so versatile as a drawing medium. With watercolor, we apply areas of pigment at varying values, so the method is based on shapes rather than collections of lines or broad strokes. Each medium requires practice with its specific techniques, but the general goals of applying value are the same.

Figure 5.5 Hatching and cross-hatching in pen and ink. Varying the density and complexity of the hatch patterns generates relative tones—the drapes at right and left, for example, are drawn with dense hatch patterns at various angles to create very dark tones.
Shop/Crit
Moscow, ID
February 4, 2009
Uniball Vision Micro in Moleskine Pocket Sketchbook (7" × 5.5")
30 minutes

In using lines for hatching, especially with ink pens, the tone should be applied consistently, without loosely scribbled marks. The lines must work together to form a tone rather than a random collection of lines, with the individual strokes of the pen or pencil being less evident than the overall pattern. This is critical to representing surfaces, volumes, and spaces. For examples of hatch patterns, see Figure 3.2. Practice building these patterns to create tones that are uniform in value (these are known as *flat tones*) as well as tones that vary gradually from dark to light and vice versa (*graded tones*). Be patient in building the tones—if you try to rush through it, the results are more likely to be sloppy, and the tones will be uneven. With large areas of hatch patterns, it can be difficult to maintain consistency of the individual lines and their spacing. Try breaking up the pattern by keeping the strokes relatively short and gathering them into groups that can be merged with other groups.

Figure 5.6   Hatching and cross-hatching in pen and ink. Even though the hatching in this case is relatively loose, its directionality is critical to the description of form.
Skidmore Fountain
Portland, OR
October 2, 2010
Copic Multiliner SP (Olive) in Moleskine Large Japanese Notebook (5" × 8")
20 minutes

The direction of the hatching is important. I generally begin hatching vertical surfaces with a vertical hatch pattern, and horizontal surfaces with a horizontal pattern. The next pattern I apply almost always attempts to reinforce the perspective. This means that the hatched lines radiate from the vanishing points of the walls or ground, whether or not the surface material has a distinct pattern (such as the horizontal lines of brick). Examples can be seen in Figure 5.1 (the lower part of the wall at left), Figure 5.5 (the hatch pattern in the ceiling), and also in Figure 7.20 (on the walls to the left and right). Applying hatch patterns in this way reinforces the sense of diminution and helps to clarify the orientation of vertical and horizontal surfaces. When reinforcing the perspective is not a factor, the second or third layer of hatching might be a simple 45° angle in either direction. Use as many patterns of opposing angles as necessary to build the required darkness of tone. Sweeping, curving stroke patterns will add surface variation and a sense of texture. They can also be used to break up the monotony that may occur if all the hatching were to be done in a rigidly consistent direction. The back wall in Figure 5.7 is an example of this technique.

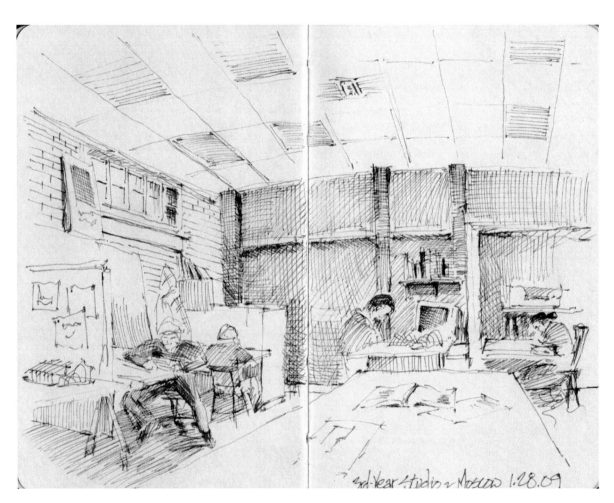

Figure 5.7   Another example of hatching and cross-hatching in pen and ink. Sweeping, curved patterns can break up the monotony of strictly vertical hatching.
Third-Year Architecture Studio
Moscow, ID
January 28, 2009
Copic Multiliner SP (Sepia) in Moleskine Pocket Sketchbook (7" × 5.5")
20 minutes

To apply value most effectively, it helps to avoid strong outlines in the setup stage. Adjacent surfaces (building corners, for example) are almost never defined by an actual line, but rather by one value meeting another along an edge. Where surfaces meet, we see a change in tone and not a dark line. With ink sketches, it can be difficult to avoid this problem. One technique is to avoid drawing outlines and instead place small dots on the page to define the ends of invisible lines on the page, but this has obvious drawbacks—it is a challenge to remember what all the dots meant when they were placed. The easier strategy is to do the setup in light pencil lines and then add value with ink. With graphite and other dry media, it is relatively easy to do the set up sketch in very light lines. When shading is added, these lines tend to disappear, leaving surfaces that are clearly defined by their relative values.

With dry media such as graphite and charcoal, once the entire drawing has been thoroughly set up with very light lines, value may be applied in two ways. You might begin at the center of focus and work your way outward, or you might work from top to bottom and/or left to right. The advantage of the latter strategy is that the sketch will more likely stay clean—your hand will not come into contact with as much graphite as you draw. In any case, feel free to rotate the page as needed so that making quick, free strokes is more comfortable, and so that your drawing hand is not likely to rub and smear the graphite already on the page.

Figure 5.8   Graphite shading that follows the vertical or horizontal direction of the building and street surfaces.
Via Bontempi
Perugia, IT
June 24, 2007
2B Pencil on Canson Drawing
Paper (9" × 12")
15 minutes

Figure 5.9 Graphite used with a broad-stroke technique to achieve smooth, even tones.
Piazza della Rotonda
Rome, IT
June 4, 2008
HB Pencil on Canson Drawing Paper (12" × 9")
30 minutes

With graphite and other dry media, it is relatively easy to create graded tones that go from light to dark, or dark to light. It is also easy to quickly create tones that vary subtly in value. This is a skill that requires practice, but it is extremely useful when trying to represent bright light and dark shadow and the subtleties of difference between the two. The sketch in Figure 5.9 relies on a fairly wide range of values to indicate the various forms and surfaces, along with the people and umbrellas. The large columns on the left required some patience in building tone that was dark enough to contrast well with the shaded facades beyond, and the lack of value on the buildings at right conveys a sense of bright sunlight. The shaded tones are very smooth—in some areas it is difficult to distinguish individual pencil strokes, and in other areas the hatching is obvious. Shading in this way shows the strength of graphite as a sketching medium—it falls between the line-based tonality of ink and the shape-oriented approach of watercolor.

Figure 5.10   A graphite sketch combining several value techniques—directional hatching, reinforcing the perspective, simplifying the value scheme, avoiding strong outlines, and increased contrast to accentuate the focus.
Vicolo delle Volpe
Rome, IT
July 5, 2007
HB Pencil on Canson Drawing Paper (9" × 12")
20 minutes

Since it is a fluid medium, applying value with watercolor requires making shapes of varying tones rather than patterns of lines. The specific techniques for applying watercolor to the page are discussed in the next chapter, but a few examples here will illustrate how this medium can be used with respect to value contrast. Strive to attain the same results with watercolor that are possible with dry media such as graphite. Although watercolor is applied with a different process, the same general strategies and goals discussed throughout this chapter will apply. Ultimately, we are trying to describe light and shade, often by directly juxtaposing both.

Figure 5.11   Watercolor.
Orfanotrofio di Santa Geltrude
Atrani, IT
June 9, 2008
Watercolor on Arches Cold Press (9" × 12")
45 minutes

The most common mistake regarding value in watercolor is to paint with weak, washed-out tones. Pale tones are necessary to describe sunlight, but these need to be contrasted against strong dark tones. In watercolor, we must use enough pigment to create these darks, but wet pigment appears darker than it will be after drying. So

Figure 5.12   Applying value with watercolor, creating a focus on the facade of the church with increased contrast and detail.
San Tommaso di Canterbury
Rome, IT
June 19, 2011
Watercolor on Arches Cold Press (9" × 12")
60 minutes

there is a tendency to hold back on the amount of pigment, resulting in weak tones after the washes have dried. The sketch in Figure 5.11 has very light values in the sky, the ground, the wall at left, and the yellow wall at the end of the path. The darks on the hillside in the distance are just dark enough to contrast well with the ornamental railing at the top of the yellow wall, while the shadows on the sloping wall at right and those on the ground are considerably darker than anything else in the view. This is the level of darkness required to create strong contrast—practice working with water and pigment combinations until you can easily achieve these values.

In Figure 5.12, though the receding street to the left is relatively dark, it is there mainly to describe the context—this small church sits alongside a piazza where the street widens. But the greatest contrast is between the church's somewhat pale facade and the very dark porthole windows. The sky is kept light enough in value so as not to compete with the shaded roof eaves, and no detail is shown on the buildings at right and left, although each had windows that were visible in this view. The focus is the church, so detail and value were accentuated in its facade and minimized elsewhere.

Be careful about the edges between opposing values in watercolor. Even if the approach of painting is relatively loose compared drawing in pen or pencil, the edges between contrasting values should be well controlled. Figure 5.13 was a quick study in watercolor, with minimal setup lines in graphite. While the brushwork is fairly relaxed, the washes do not bleed into one another—the edges are crisp and the adjacent values are distinct. Be patient in waiting for washes to dry completely before adding a darker value on top of a lighter one, or immediately adjacent to it, especially when a clear contrast is needed.

Figure 5.13   There is less detail and precision in this sketch than that achieved in Figure 5.15, though the subject is the same. In both cases, the value contrast is strong and clear.
Temple of Ceres
Paestum, IT
June 10, 2011
Watercolor in Moleskine Large Watercolor Sketchbook (8" × 5")
25 minutes

Contrast and Counterpoint

Value is relative—the way we perceive a particular value has to do with adjacent values. Baroque painters of the early 17th century made very effective use of value contrast by using a technique known as *chiaroscuro*, an Italian term that literally means "clear/obscure" and that roughly translates as "light/dark." A more dramatic form of chiaroscuro is called *tenebroso*, meaning "dark" or "murky." In sketching, the strategy is known as *counterpoint*.

Figure 5.14   Counterpoint, or light against dark in this case, brings out the edges of the whitewashed architecture against the landscape background.
Comunale San Sebastiano
Atrani, IT
June 7, 2008
2B Pencil on Canson Classic Cream Drawing Paper (9" × 12")
30 minutes

Directly juxtaposing light against dark has the effect of intensifying each—the light will appear to be lighter, and the dark, darker. These strategies for representing light and shade lead to a stronger sense of visual drama in a painting or sketch. They have the effect of exciting the viewer's eye—there is a stronger visual response to a well-contrasted image than to an image where all the values are similar to one another.

Counterpoint is one of the most important considerations when adding value to a sketch, as it creates clear distinctions between surfaces and objects in space. Simplifying the value scheme will often lead to sketches with counterpoint elements. But even in sketches with relatively complex value schemes, you should look for opportunities to employ the technique because it can make a two-dimensional sketch appear to project into the third dimension. It is surprising how suddenly an object can change from being light against a dark background to dark against a light background. A simple example is shown in Figure 5.14, with the light-toned architecture placed against a dark background of landscape elements. The background was not quite so dark in reality, but has been exaggerated to emphasize the three-dimensional distinction between the objects in space. A more complex approach to counterpoint is seen in Figure 5.15, specifically in the wooden railing that surrounds the temple. Where the railing is against a dark background at left, it is kept very light. When it is seen against a light background at the base of the temple, the railing is drawn as dark. Although the actual value of the railing was essentially the same in reality, its value changes relative to the value of the background.

Figure 5.15   The same temple as that in Figure 5.13, sketched from almost the same point of view, showing the use of counterpoint in the wooden railing.
Temple of Ceres
Paestum, IT
June 12, 2009
2B Pencil on Canson Drawing Paper (12" × 9")
40 minutes

Figure 5.16   Counterpoint applied to columns.
The Pantheon
Rome, IT
July 6, 2011
2B Pencil on Canson Classic Cream Drawing Paper (12" × 9")
60 minutes

Figure 5.16 shows another example of counterpoint, and reveals that the shift from light-against-dark to dark-against-light can happen very suddenly. The columns across the front of the building did not vary greatly in value, but their background shifted quickly from dark to light, so the value of the columns had to be sketched accordingly. The brightly sunlit buildings beyond the three columns at far right required the columns to be drawn as dark against light. The shaded area behind the next three columns to the left required that these columns remain light. The very tops of the second and third columns from the right also had to remain light against their shaded background. When we look closely at these sudden differences in value, it might look odd or "incorrect." But if we step back slightly and look at the sketch as a whole, the counterpoint works to suggest light and depth of space.

Forced Shadows and Reflected Light

Drawing on the principle of counterpoint, light and shade may be strongly emphasized through a technique known as *forcing shadows*. When we look at a shadow, the initial impression might be that its tone is uniform throughout, that the shadow's entire shape is a single, dark tone. In fact, virtually all shadows contain some variation in value—some areas are lighter or darker than others. It may be difficult to see this variation at first glance, and even upon further study, significant variation might not be apparent. The differences may seem to be too subtle to bother with in trying to make a sketch. However, although the tonal variation of shadows may be slight, by forcing the shadows we can create a more accurate representation of how light behaves. Rather than sketching shadows as though their value is entirely uniform, apply a graded tone, with the darkest part at the leading edge of the shadow. Placing the darkest area of the shadow directly adjacent to the sunlit surface will have the effect of enhancing both values. As the shadow moves away from its leading edge—that is, deeper into the shadow and further from the light—it is common to observe some light that has been reflected from the street or other building surfaces. So, by grading the shadow away from its edge, and making it lighter, two things happen. First, the darker edge of the shadow will contrast more forcefully with the adjacent sunlit surface. And second, the graded shadow will represent reflected light bouncing off of other surfaces. An example can be seen in Figure 5.16, in the shadows cast by the cornices along the left side of the building. These shadows have a strong, clear edge where they meet the sunlit surface of the wall, and they are graded to a lighter value as they wrap around the cylindrical face of the structure.

Figure 5.17 Forced shadows on the facades along the left side of the street.
Via del Teatro Valle
Rome, IT
May 24, 2011
4B Pencil on Canson Drawing Paper
(9" × 12")
45 minutes

Figure 5.17 is another good example of forced shadows, especially along the left side of the street in view. The leading edge of the shadow is sketched with darkness and precision, modeling the columns of the facade at left. This shadow becomes lighter as it moves downward, away from the shadow's leading edge. This sketch also shows increased contrast as a way to draw attention to the central focus of the sketch—the triangular pediment at upper left and the spiral church lantern beyond. Notice that this lantern is sketched with slightly lighter

Figure 5.18   Counterpoint and reflected light on the wall at right.
San Salvatore da Birecto
Atrani, IT
June 13, 2009
4B Pencil on Canson Classic Cream Drawing Paper (9" × 12")
50 minutes

value and reduced contrast. While it is a major focus of the sketch, the lantern is at a greater distance, so it is drawn with less crispness than the triangular pediment. This is sometimes referred to as *atmospheric perspective* because it shows objects at a distance as if through the haze of the atmosphere. It has greater impact in views that show significant distance, but even in a sketch like this, it can be a useful device.

An example that combines counterpoint and reflected light can be seen in Figure 5.18. In this case, the left wall of the building on the right deserves special attention. The wall was in shade, so the corner closest to the viewer had to show a shaded surface meeting a sunlit surface. To the right of the corner, the wall is left as the white of the paper, and to the left of the corner the surface is shaded. However, the landscape beyond this building, visible to the right of the small clock tower, was considerably darker than even the darkest part of the shaded wall. Also, there was significant light being reflected off the face of the clock tower and the buildings to the left. So the shaded wall required a carefully graded tone to represent all of these factors. Also note the railing atop the building at right—this was a small study in counterpoint, shifting as it does from dark-against-light at the corner to light-against-dark to the right and left.

Material and Detail as Value

In drawing detail or building materials, always consider the effect this will have on value. Material such as brick or stone and details such as window shutters can easily become a tone—some version of gray—rather than accurately representing the intended subject. So it's important to either sketch these elements without unintentionally putting down a wash of gray on the page, or to leave them out in favor of a sketch with clear values. As a general rule, if the material is quite close to the observer and important to the view, it should be sketched. If it is at even a slight distance and is in full sunlight, or if it is not critical to the view, it should be sketched with the very faintest of marks or avoided entirely. In Figure 5.19, the character of the stone wall on the right was important to describing the scene—the streets of Assisi are partially defined by the texture of their walls. The small buttress on the wall at left and the walls beyond were also made of stone, but at this distance it would be too difficult to draw the stone in the same way as the wall on the right, and such fine detail would not have helped the sketch. If the stone were sketched on the buttress, and beyond, it would have created a gray tone that would not have worked well with the value in the rest of the sketch.

When sketching the materials of a surface is desirable, do not sketch it as patches—that is, with a small patch of material here and another there. This has the effect of making the surface look as though it has large dirty spots on it because the patches of rendered material will appear as areas of tone. To avoid having to apply materials to entire surfaces, the material may be gradually faded out from one edge to another, especially as its distance from the observer increases. The sketch in Figure 5.20 shows crumbled, worn brick on the walls of ruins at Ostia, IT. Even though the brick was in bright sunlight, my proximity to the wall required some suggestion of texture, but this needed to be very limited so as not to create too dark a tone. But the material is not shown as patches. In some cases, there were pockets where the brick had broken away, and these were represented with shadows. But the overall handling of the material is consistent.

Often, the best strategy is to only show material if it is in shade. If a surface is in full sunlight, consider leaving it alone in the sketch—for example, do not draw the bricks on a sunlit brick wall, so that the wall remains as light as possible (the white of the page). In Figure 5.21, the building was constructed with multicolored brick, but trying to render this material on the sunlit surfaces would have created gray tones, preventing clear contrast between light and shade. The shaded areas, on the other hand, offered the opportunity to suggest the material pattern in the way the value was applied. The darker-colored bricks are picked out in the shading, and their directionality reinforces the perspective.

Figure 5.19 The stone wall at right was close enough to carefully sketch the material. Treating the small buttress at left (and anything further away) in the same way would have created an unwanted value.
Via di Monte Cavallo
Assisi, IT
June 27, 2009
Soft Charcoal Pencil on Canson Drawing Paper (9" × 12")
25 minutes

Figure 5.20 Worn and broken brick on ancient ruins. The rendering of material is kept very light and consistent, though even with this light touch, the material begins to read as a tone.
Ostia Antica
Rome, IT
May 30, 2008
HB and 2B Pencil on Canson Classic Cream Drawing Paper (9" × 12")
40 minutes

BEROL 314 45 MIN.   CASCADE HALL 5/6/03

Figure 5.21 Showing material in the shaded areas and keeping the sunlit surfaces as light as possible.
Cascade Hall, University of Oregon
Eugene, OR
May 6, 2003
Berol 314 Pencil in Pro-Art Sketchbook (5.5" × 8")
45 minutes

Details such as windows and doors should be sketched lightly at first, with darker marks being added in order to suggest only strongly shaded spots. Even if the shutters in a view are dark colored, for example, focus more on the lines of darkness created by the louvers or the shadow cast on the wall behind. In sketching details like this, there is a tendency to stamp them out, one after another, in exactly the same way. This will lead to a

Figure 5.22 Avoid making repeated details, such as windows, all the same. Even small variations from one to another will create a livelier image.
Piazza di Sant'Ignazio
Rome, IT
July 8, 2007
HB Pencil on Canson Drawing Paper (12" × 9")
45 minutes

dull sketch that lacks variety. Look carefully at repeating elements—windows are the best example—and see how they differ from one another. This window might have its shutters closed, that one might have its drapes open, another might be completely open, etc. Even if they look similar at first glance, try to avoid drawing them all as being identical. Figure 5.22 is a worthwhile effort in value for several reasons—shifting tones that describe building form, forced shadows that create strong contrast and suggest reflected light, directional hatching that reinforces the perspective, etc. But it is included here especially because it shows enough variety in the window treatment as to be worth studying.

Color and Value

Value contrast is not only about light and dark. Different colors will react to one another and further accentuate the rendering of light and shade in a sketch. The next chapter will cover some of the elements of color compliments and color temperature, but a few points with regard to value are appropriate here. When working in color, it is just as important to keep the value scheme relatively simple, and to apply the other strategies discussed in this chapter. Color can confuse the issue of value, so in some ways it helps to simplify values even more than you would with dry media. An example is shown in Figure 5.23. The focus is clearly on the obelisk, its pedestal, and the fragment of ancient sculpture to the right. The landscape beyond was not so much darker

6.1.11   Villa Celimontana

Figure 5.23   Despite the variety of color in this sketch, the value contrast is very clear.
Obelisk in Villa Celimontana
Rome, IT
June 1, 2011
Watercolor in in Moleskine Large Watercolor
Sketchbook (5" × 8")
40 minutes

than these elements, so I had to strategize on value before beginning the sketch. In an effort to bring out the focal elements, and especially the obelisk, the landscape was given a deep, dark value in greens and blues. The obelisk was colored stone (with the top half being a darker type of stone), but this color still had to be kept very light in relation to the foliage in the background. The pedestal was kept as light as possible, and I was careful to edge the steps in white, to maintain separation between these and the landscape beyond. So, even though this was a colorful sketch, the main strategy had to do with simple value contrast.

Figure 5.24 The color of shadows tends to be based on the color of the surfaces they are cast upon.
Vicolo del Bologna
Rome, IT
July 6, 2010
Watercolor in Moleskine Large Watercolor Sketchbook (5" × 8")
25 minutes

Vicolo del Bologna 7.6.10

In most cases, the color of a shadow tends to be the same color as the surface it is being cast upon. The shadow is a stronger, more saturated version of the surface color, but they generally have the same hue. So if a sunlit surface is a very pale blue, the surface in shade will be the same blue at much higher saturation—and the higher the saturation of most colors, the darker their value. Though it is a very quick and loose sketch, Figure 5.24 illustrates this point. The shadow on the reddish-orange building at the far end of the street is a darker version of the same color in sunlight. The central yellowish building is shaded with a richer, darker, yellowish-brown—and a small amount of blue that forces the shadow's edge.

Rua da Bica   7.22.11

Figure 5.25   Contrasted color
temperatures, cool and warm, will
further accentuate the sense of
light and dark in a sketch.
Rua da Bica
Lisbon, PT
July 22, 2011
Watercolor in Moleskine Large
Watercolor Sketchbook (5" × 8")
30 minutes

Another issue with regard to color and value is that surfaces in full sun will appear warmer, and surfaces in shade will appear cooler. The dark blue and purple tones in Figure 5.25 contrast with the warmer yellows, reds, and oranges, creating a sense of bright sunlight and deep shade. Notice also the direction of the brush strokes—horizontal or vertical, depending on the orientation of the surface.

In applying value, keep in mind the strategies discussed in this chapter. Rely on media-specific techniques and bring everything together to project a clear sense of light and depth of space. This will result in compelling sketches that communicate the dramatic character of space and form as revealed by the sun.

CHAPTER

6 *COLOR*

When a sketch has been set up effectively, value can create a clear sense of light, depth, and texture. Color, whether it is added as value or in addition to value, can add a richer sense of vitality, creating a more dynamic representation of the view. There are a variety of ways to add color to a sketch, and, of course, color may be used alone. Of the numerous types of media that might be used for sketching—including markers, pastels, acrylics, etc.—my focus is on two types of media that travel well and that are quite simple and direct in their application. Colored pencil is recommended particularly as a means of learning how to mix colors, and watercolor because it is uniquely suited to sketching quickly on location. Each requires fundamental skills and both can be used to produce accurate and compelling results. Regardless of the color techniques you use, it is important to continue the same approach to value discussed in the preceding chapter. Don't allow color sketches become "washed-out" for lack of value contrast. Color should not be seen as a substitute for value— whether it is added to a sketch that has already been given value, or if color is the way that value will be added, in either case, strong value contrast should always be present.

Figure 6.1 A richly colored sketch that maintains a clear sense of light through strong value contrast.
Rua das Portas
Lisbon, PT
July 22, 2011
Watercolor on Winsor & Newton Cotman Cold Press (9" × 12")
30 minutes

Figure 6.2 A simple pen and ink sketch, with the addition of one color (Alizarin Crimson).
La Ria Taberna
Barcelona, SP
July 2, 2009
Uniball Vision Micro and Watercolor in Moleskine Large Watercolor Sketchbook (8" × 5")
20 minutes

Starting Simply

The best way to begin working with color is, very simply, by adding only one or two colors to a sketch that has already been completed (through the steps of setup and value) in pen or pencil. Adding just one color can effectively draw attention to an interesting element of the view and it makes the process direct and uncomplicated. In Figure 6.2, I was sitting at a tavern in Barcelona that had a window behind the bar that was open to the street outside. It was an interesting spatial situation, with people occasionally walking up to the window to order a beer or to chat with the bartender. I had finished the sketch in pen, but felt that something was lacking. The focus of the sketch was the window, and it was this element of the view that drove me to do the sketch in the first place. The window frame was an intense, deep red, so I quickly pulled out my watercolor palette and in less than a minute's time I had transformed a worthwhile sketch into something far more compelling and memorable.

Figure 6.3   Completed the same day as the sketch in Figure 6.2. I was in a mood to work with color in a simple way and had the foresight to take photos of each sketch before adding the color. In this case, the colors were Cerulean Blue and Gamboge.
La Pedrera
Barcelona, SP
July 2, 2009
Copic Multiliner SP (Sepia) and Watercolor in Moleskine Large Watercolor Sketchbook (5" × 8")
30 minutes

Wells Fargo &
The Red Door
Moscow, ID 11·21·09

Figure 6.4   In this sketch, just two points of color highlight an otherwise simple pen and ink sketch. Alizarin Crimson and Gamboge were the only pigments used to call attention to the bank's sign on the left and the restaurant's door on the right.
Wells Fargo and The Red Door
Moscow, ID
November 21, 2009
Uniball Vision Micro and Watercolor in Moleskine Pocket Sketchbook (7" × 5.5")
20 minutes

   Another simple way to begin working with color is to create monochromatic sketches in a medium other than graphite or black ink. Working in monochrome—that is, a single color for the entire sketch—is excellent practice, because it keeps the focus on value. Sketching in graphite or charcoal is working in monochrome, so the same strategies will apply. Colored pencils in earth tones work very well for this purpose—my favorite colors are Venetian Red, Chocolate, and Terra Cotta, all produced by the Derwent company.

Figure 6.5   A monochromatic sketch in colored pencil, using Venetian Red.
Colosseum
Rome, IT
July 10, 2011
Derwent Venetian Red Pencil on Canson Drawing Paper (9" × 9")
45 minutes

    While making the shift to watercolor, it is advisable to work with a single color for some time, to develop an ability to mix the appropriate amounts of water and pigment in order to achieve distinct values. When full color is used from the start, there is a tendency to ignore value. This type of training will lead to values that are dark enough to serve as contrast when you are trying to represent bright sunlight.

Figure 6.6   Monochromatic watercolor made as practice for mixing and applying washes of varying value. (Study made after a photograph of the William E. Martin House by Frank Lloyd Wright; Oak Park, IL)

Colored Pencil

Colored pencils can be used effectively to add color to a sketch, especially if the setup is first completed using pen and ink. But the primary reason colored pencils are included here is because they are an excellent way to learn how to mix colors. Working with colored pencils requires a slower, more methodical approach than using watercolor. It shows more clearly the effects of blending various colors without sacrificing strong value contrast. Starting with the three primary colors, and learning to mix them on the page, gives an excellent sense of working with color that will build a foundation for working in watercolor. To mix colored pencils properly, you must be able to apply color to the page very evenly, one color at a time. A consistent hatch pattern works well, making marks in both directions—back and forth—as you go. The most important factor is even distribution—be sure that the value is consistent and that there is little or no white paper showing when you are done. Practice applying the color in a variety of value strengths, from very light to very dark. A basic value scale in colored pencil is shown in Figure 6.7. The lightest value is the white of the paper. The darkest is made by applying enough pressure to leave strong marks, but not so much as to obliterate the paper's texture or leave a waxy buildup on the page. The three values between these two ends of the spectrum should be evenly distributed in terms of their value.

Figure 6.7   Basic values in colored pencil. Full strength is at far right, medium strength is in the center.

There are a few different ways to make marks with colored pencil, but in all cases, the goal should be consistent coverage on the paper. This consistency is needed for the colors to blend well and evenly when the time comes to mix them. It helps to practice a variety of mark patterns, especially in graded tones, as is seen in Figure 6.8. The first pattern on the left is called *scumbling*, which is making very small marks in an even distribution. The pattern at the far right consists of larger random strokes and the three patterns in the center are variations of hatch patterns. In all cases, the goal is to create an evenly graded tone, without a noticeable imbalance between color and the white of the page. In making graded tones with colored pencil, it is usually easiest to work from light to dark. Begin with a very light touch, making a value no darker than the second square from the left in Figure 6.7. Strive for a smooth transition as you increase pressure and try to achieve the proper value in a single pass, rather than going over an area more than once in an effort to make it darker. Once you begin to feel comfortable making a variety of distinct and graded values, then move on to the next step of making a color wheel.

Figure 6.8   Graded values with colored pencil, using various stroke patterns.

There are varying points of view on color theory, and what should be considered "primary colors," but for our purposes we mean some version of blue, red, and yellow. With Prismacolor brand pencils, the specific colors I use are named *True Blue*, *Magenta*, and *Canary Yellow*, and these are what were used to create the color wheel below. I recommend starting with these colors, but variations of blues, reds, and yellows can produce interesting results. For example, a darker palette might consist of Ultramarine in place of True Blue, Scarlet Lake for the Magenta, and Goldenrod to replace the Yellow. More important than the specific primary colors is their handling and application as you mix two or more primaries to create other colors.

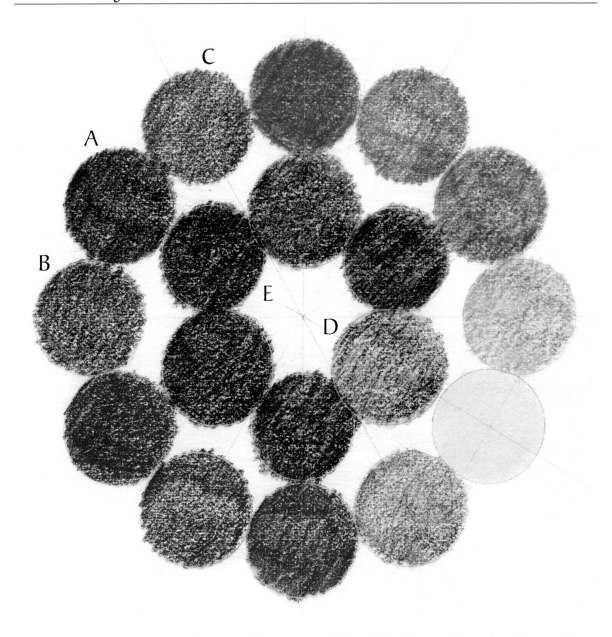

Figure 6.9   Color wheel in colored pencil, using True Blue, Magenta, and Canary Yellow. Primary and secondary colors are in the outer ring of circles, with tertiary colors in the inner ring.

A simple color wheel is shown in Figure 6.9, and in the process of making one you will learn much about mixing colors. The circle at top center is filled with True Blue at full strength, corresponding in value to the square at far right in Figure 6.7. The circle at lower left is full strength Magenta and at lower right is full strength Canary Yellow. Around the outer ring of the wheel, between each pair of the primary colors, are three circles of secondary colors, which are a combination of the two adjacent primaries. The three circles at upper left, between Magenta and True Blue, combine these two colors at varying strength. The middle circle ("A") is a blend of True Blue and Magenta, both at full strength. The circle at "B" is full strength Magenta

Figure 6.10 Recreating colors from strips of magazine pages, pasted to drawing paper. This is an excellent practice technique for training your eye to see how tertiary colors can be composed of the three primaries.

Figure 6.11 Colored pencil applied to a sketch, using only the three primary colors.
Vicolo della Torre
Rome, IT
May 26, 2011
Uniball Vision Micro and Colored Pencil in Moleskine Large Watercolor Sketchbook (5" × 8")
25 minutes

and half strength True Blue (with "half strength" corresponding to the middle square in Figure 6.7), and the circle at "C" is full strength True Blue and half strength Magenta. The same pattern is repeated between True Blue and Canary Yellow, and between Canary Yellow and Magenta. By mixing the three primaries in this way, nine distinct secondary colors can be created—making for a total of twelve colors around the outer ring of the wheel. The circles in the wheel's inner ring are filled with tertiary colors, which have this name because they combine all three primaries. The circle at "D" combines full strength Canary Yellow with half strength Magenta and True Blue, and the circle at "E" combines full strength Magenta and True Blue with half strength Canary Yellow.

A good way to practice color mixing is shown in Figure 6.10. Cut strips from magazines, and paste them down to a sheet of drawing paper. The strips should show an assortment of colors without much detail. Try to extend the colors and patterns from the magazine strips onto the drawing paper, using only the three primary colored pencils. The example on the left shows how the colors are constructed, starting with a layer of True Blue, followed by Magenta, and finally Canary Yellow. Up close, you will see bits of the three primaries, so it is sometimes necessary to step back from the drawing, or to blur your eyes slightly, to see how the colors are blending. With practice, your will develop a good sense of how to build virtually any tertiary color, at any value, using only the three primary colors.

While I don't often sketch in colored pencil as the sole medium, occasionally it's an easy way to add color to a sketch that has been set up in ink (Figure 6.11). This approach is perhaps less complicated than using watercolor because it doesn't require as much specialized equipment. With just three pencils, any color can be applied to the sketch. However, it can be a slower process than working with watercolor, because three layers of pencil are required to create the colors, so the same area must be colored three times to achieve the desired result. Using the three primaries in colored pencils as the sole medium for a sketch, it can be difficult to create values dark enough to represent strong light contrast. Adding Black colored pencil can help in this effort, though this further extends the time required to fully develop the drawing.

KIBBIE DOME   30MIN.   9.24.04

Figure 6.12   Colored pencil as the primary medium, with the addition of Black colored pencil for stronger dark values.
Kibbie Dome
Moscow, ID
September 24, 2004
Colored Pencil in Pro-Art Sketchbook (8" × 6")
30 minutes

Watercolor

Watercolor, as a fluid medium, is one of the quickest and most versatile media for applying color when sketching on location. Even if you only have a few colors on your palette—typically, one version each of blue, red, and yellow—the possibilities are endless with regard to color and value. It is a transparent medium (as opposed to gouache, oil, or acrylic, which are opaque), capable of producing dazzling results with respect to light and depth. After mastering some basic techniques for handling water, pigment, and brushwork, this medium can be used to swiftly apply color and value. With watercolor, it can be a challenge to sketch with precision. But the medium lends itself to a more abstract approach based on impressions of light, color, and texture. For example, the sketch in Figure 6.13 gives a rather loose impression of the colorful flowers beneath the canopy of canvas umbrellas. The colors are pure and clean, though working with a brush prevents the type of crisp detail that is possible with graphite or ink.

To develop strong fundamental skills with watercolor, it helps to start with relatively small sketches. Fragments of views sketched as quick vignettes are more manageable than large paintings and they are a low-impact way to test strategies and procedures for painting. This approach is also worthwhile if you have not used watercolor in some time. The three quick sketches shown in Figure 6.14 are a good example—I had not used

Figure 6.13 A quick watercolor sketch with fresh colors and strong value contrast.
Campo dei Fiori
Rome, IT
June 22, 2010
Watercolor in Moleskine Large Watercolor Sketchbook (5" × 8")
20 minutes

watercolor for a few months, so I painted these fragments as a way to re-familiarize myself with the process and get warmed-up before attempting larger subjects. I sometimes find that when I try to take on too much with watercolor, the process can be frustrating rather than relaxing and enjoyable. It's better to work up to larger-format sketches instead of trying to tackle a large subject from the start. Small sketches of this type also have the benefit of exercising the eye in terms of color and value, while still taking on the relative complexity of working with a variety of colors.

Figure 6.14   Small fragmentary views are an excellent way to practice in the field. Each of these studies is just about 2" or 3" square and only took a few minutes.
Portico d'Ottavia and Vicinity
Rome, IT
June 3, 2010
Watercolor on Arches Cold Press (12" × 9")
5 minutes each

Another strategy for starting small and simple is to eliminate elements of the view that would significantly increase the complexity of the sketch. In Figure 6.15, I eliminated the buildings in the background so that I could focus on the statue as the sole subject matter. Ordinarily, I would have included the buildings to give a more complete sense of the context. In this case, omitting them allowed me to focus only on the statue and to keep the process of painting as simple as possible, partially by minimizing the number of colors required for the sketch.

Even before attempting small studies such as these, though, it's very important to practice basic skills for applying watercolor to a blank page. Watercolor is an extremely versatile medium, with a multitude of techniques and resulting visual effects. There are all sorts of techniques for applying color—splattering with the brush or other devices (such as toothbrushes and sponges), adding other liquids or materials such as salt to the wash for mottled effects, and applying frisket or other masking fluid to prevent areas from being colored (the masking fluid dries in a film layer on the page, and after painting, it is rubbed or peeled off to reveal the white of the paper). Any of these and many other techniques may yield interesting results, but, for at least two reasons, I strongly recommend mastering basic techniques that do not require any special materials or equipment. The first reason has to do with keeping your approach to sketching as simple and direct as possible. Working on location is far easier, and thus more likely to happen when the opportunity arises, if you

Figure 6.15 Keeping the sketch simple by omitting elements, such as the buildings that were in the background of this view.
Monument to Giordano Bruno
Rome, IT
July 10, 2009
Watercolor in Moleskine Large Watercolor Sketchbook (5" × 8")
25 minutes

don't need to carry a large assortment of tools and materials. The second reason is that an amazing array of effects can be produced with only the most basic techniques. The only way to discover the possibilities with a minimum of tools and techniques is to spend a good amount of time using only these tools and techniques. Eventually you may feel the need to diversify your toolkit or attempt more complex methods of painting, but these advanced steps will be more valuable if they are built on strong foundational skills. Personally, after many years of working with watercolor, I am still making discoveries and mastering my own skills with only the most basic tools and techniques. These include flat, graded, glazed, and wet-into-wet washes, and dry-brush and calligraphic techniques.

Figure 6.16   Watercolor brush with a bead of water applied to the page. Only the very tip of the brush should be touching the page, just enough to move the bead of water and pigment.

A "wash" is an area of color applied to the paper that does not show brush strokes. A flat wash is an area of a single color with uniform value. Practicing flat washes will help you learn how to work with water, pigment, and brushes. It's the most fundamental of watercolor techniques, so practice this until it becomes easy, quick, and comfortable to achieve consistent results. To make a flat wash, mix some water and pigment on the palette. "Load" or "charge" the brush so that it is full of the water/pigment mix without quite dripping. Touch just the tip of the brush to the page and begin to move the bead of water and pigment. Do not press down on the brush—use the brush only to move the water, and let the water distribute the pigment (Figure 6.16). Keep the bead of water moving, spreading the wash evenly across the page. It can help to tilt the page slightly so that the bead of water remains at the leading edge of the wash. When the brush begins to empty, reload it with more of the water/pigment mix. When applying a flat wash, you should never feel the need to press down on the brush to apply the pigment to the page—if you do, then the brush likely needs to be recharged. When you come to the point where the wash should stop, there will be a surplus of water in the bead. Snap out the excess water from the brush with a quick downward arm motion (the water/pigment will splatter on the ground), then touch the tip of the brush to the excess water on the page. The brush will act as a vacuum and remove the bead at the edge of the wash. Until the wash dries completely, do not try to "touch it up" in any way. Brushing the paper while it is wet with a wash will tend to dissolve the fibers of the paper's surface and create splotchy, uneven areas of color.

If you have applied a flat wash properly, there will be a clear, even area of pigment on the page (Figure 6.17). Notice that washes will become lighter in value as they dry. A common mistake is to mix a wash with the desired value when it is wet, only to find that the wash is not as strongly valued after drying. Be sure to mix enough water and pigment before beginning a large wash so that you don't run out before completing it, especially if the consistency of color and value are important in a particular situation. It's not usually a problem to have some

Figure 6.17   A simple flat wash. No significant variations in color or value are visible and there is no evidence of any brush strokes.

Figure 6.18   Franning happens when a newly applied wash creeps into a partially dried wash already on the page.

minor variation in value and color, but it is a problem if you have to take time to recreate a similar wash on the palette while the wash on the page is drying. This may lead to a noticeable break in the wash, from one color and value to another. It can also create a problem known as *fanning* or *blooming*. This happens when one wash creeps into another that has already been applied to the page (Figure 6.18). This may be used intentionally as a technique for particular effect, but in my work it's usually a mistake, something I didn't intend to do. Nevertheless, these "mistakes" can often turn out to be blessings in disguise—frustrating in the moment, but effective in the end. The sky in Figure 6.27 is an example of unintentional fanning that created an interesting result.

A glazed wash is simply one flat wash being applied over another that has been given time to dry completely. If you use the same color for the glazing wash as you did for the first wash, the value will be increased. By applying multiple layers, a variety of values may be achieved from a single mix of water and pigment (Figure 6.19). Glazing can also be done with different colors, but the succeeding layers need to be of relatively transparent pigments so that the previous layer can show through. A light yellow wash over a light blue wash, for example, will produce a green.

Figure 6.19   A glazed wash of the same pigment and value. At left is one layer of the wash, in the center are two layers, and at right there are three.

A graded wash is an area of a single color with varying value, going gradually from dark to light or vice versa. It is usually easier to go from a dark to a light value, but it's worthwhile to practice both techniques. Start with a pigment-rich wash on the palette and begin to paint as if applying a flat wash—use the tip of the brush to move the bead of water across the page. As the brush begins to lose its charge, dip it in fresh water and add this to the wash on the palette, diluting the mix slightly. Then continue to apply the wash with the diluted mix. Repeat this procedure as you go and the wash will lighten in value as the ratio of water to pigment increases. It takes some practice to master this technique without producing broken washes, where there is an obvious shift from one value to another. The change in value should be as gradual as possible—the yellow and red at far left in Figure 6.20 are excellent examples of graded washes. This technique can be very useful, especially as a way of forcing shadows and for shifting surfaces from light-against-dark to dark-against-light, as discussed in the previous chapter titled "Value."

Graded washes are a simple way to create value variation on the page. They can also be used to create color variation—try the same process, but instead of adding water, gradually add a wash of a different color. Variations in value and color can enliven watercolor sketches—if every wash is flat, the overall sketch might be a bit flat as well. An excellent way to bring variation to washes on the page is a wet-into-wet technique. Begin by applying a wash of clear water on the page. Before it begins to dry, introduce a drop or two of a pigmented wash and allow the color to migrate freely into the clear water wash. By allowing the water and pigment merge and flow across the

Figure 6.20   Graded washes with a variety of pigments. Some of these are more successful than others. The blue at bottom center, for example, suffers from a broken wash and some fanning.

Figure 6.21   Wet-into-wet washes with multiple colors. Water was applied to the page, and pigment was added before the water had dried. This is a good technique to practice mixing colors on the page.

page, interesting effects can be produced. Try tilting the page to move the pigment in different directions, and use an empty brush to remove excess water at the edge of the wash. After practicing this technique, and learning how to control a wet-into-wet wash, try the same strategy with two washes of different colors. This will produce washes in which the colors remain distinct in some areas while merging in others to create variety and texture (Figure 6.21).

Most work in watercolor consists of applying flat washes of colors that have been thoroughly mixed on the palette. But if this is the only method used for painting, the resulting sketches will often lack depth and variety. Some variation in a wash's component color is desirable and a variation of the wet-into-wet approach can help make this happen. I generally try to avoid fully mixed, perfectly uniform washes of color whenever possible, and instead try to let the colors blend on the page. If they are not fully blended into a single color, the result will be more representative of the variations we observe in virtually every view. Seeing the component colors has the effect of exciting the viewer's eye, similar to the effect of mixing colors with colored pencil. When a yellow and a blue are thoroughly mixed before they are applied to the page, the result will be a uniform green. If they are partially mixed, we will see a green that is more blue in some areas and more yellow in others. When the component colors are visible, the resulting color is usually more vibrant and interesting, pulsing with multiple colors rather than lying flatly on the page. Experiment by only partially combining two colored washes on the palette, and as the wash is being applied to the page, recharge the brush in alternating fashion from one color to the other.

In addition to these wash techniques, there are a few simple ways to use the brush that will extend the possibilities for sketching in watercolor. One is a dry-brush technique. Start with a brush that is lightly loaded with a water-and-pigment mix. Drag the side of the brush against the page, and the roughness of the paper will only pick up some of the pigment, producing a textured effect (Figure 6.23). This can be a good way to break up a flat wash, or to fade-out the edges of a wash, or to suggest rough surfaces. An example can be seen on the right wall in Figure 6.26, but this brush technique can be applied in many situations.

Figure 6.22 Component colors being blended as the wash is applied to the page. This can be seen most clearly in the wall on the left—the component colors in this case are Burnt Sienna and Sepia. The sky is a more standard wet-into-wet wash, with Cerulean Blue being added to a clear water wash on the page.
Via della Scala
Rome, IT
July 6, 2010
Watercolor on Arches Cold Press (9" × 12")
60 minutes

Figure 6.23   Dry-brush technique, useful for applying textural qualities to a watercolor sketch.

Another useful brush technique is similar to calligraphy. Again, the brush should be relatively dry as you use it to draw lines and curves that vary in width. A good #6 Round brush will come to a point when it is lightly snapped, removing most of the water/pigment mixture, and allowing for fairly thin lines to be made. Use calligraphic strokes to represent trees and their branches, overhead power lines, linear building elements, and any other part of a view that requires more of a drawing technique as opposed to a wash. In painting trees like those in Figure 6.24, try to vary the color and value as you go along, to avoid a flat appearance.

Regardless of the wash techniques you use, always strive to keep the water in the reservoir as clean as possible. If you paint a wash with nothing but this water, and the wash can be seen after drying (usually a light gray or brown), then the water should be replaced. If the water is not absolutely clear, every wash will be at least slightly more dull or muddy than it needs to be. Since it is so easy to replenish your reservoir as often as

Figure 6.24   Calligraphic brushwork used for trees and other details, made with a single #6 Round brush.
Friendship Square
Moscow, ID
February 27, 2010
Watercolor in Moleskine Large Watercolor Sketchbook (16" × 5")
45 minutes

needed, there is no reason to work with cloudy water. There is also a simple technique that can help to keep the water clean as you go along. When your brush contains pigment, and you'd like to clean it without muddying the reservoir, first snap the brush downward to whip out the excess water and pigment. Then put just the tip of the brush in the reservoir, and the brush will soak up fresh water. Immediately snap the brush again, removing the water and more of the pigment. Repeat this several times, until both your brush and your water are free of pigment. Just be sure that no one is standing too close, and that nothing around you is in danger of being splattered by paint.

Representing color can be similar to value in that it sometimes needs to be exaggerated or slightly oversimplified to avoid a sketch that is too uniform in hue and tone. The "temperature" of the colors can significantly add to the sense of value contrast. Cool colors placed next to warm colors will enhance the contrasts in value, making the lights appear lighter and the darks appear darker. In most cases, surfaces that are exposed to direct sunlight will appear to be relatively warm in color, while shaded surfaces will be cool. This contrast can be emphasized by working with color compliments. Keep sunlit surfaces very light in value

Figure 6.25   By making the shadows cool colors, relative to warm colors in sunlight, the color contrast helps to emphasize the value of each.
Tempio di Sant'Angelo
Perugia, IT
June 25, 2011
Watercolor in on Arches Cold Press (12" × 9")
45 minutes

and try to use the warmer colors on your palette—yellows, reds, oranges, ochres, etc. Shaded areas should be painted quite dark (especially where the edge of a shadow meets the sunlight), and with cool colors—mainly blues and purples.

In terms of value, I always work from the lightest to the darkest washes. One reason for this strategy is that you can always go over a light wash and make it darker with another wash—that is, making a layered or glazed wash. But once a dark wash has dried on the page, it can be very difficult or even impossible to make it lighter. Another benefit is that your water will remain relatively clean when you are laying down light washes that should be as clear and pure in color as possible. Begin by determining what will be the lightest areas of the sketch—it is often best if these areas are retained as the white of the page, as this is the very lightest value possible. If they do receive a wash, keep it very diluted in order to maintain the sense of bright sunlight. Be patient and allow the light washes dry completely before adding darker washes, or the darker pigment will spread into the light wash. To avoid spending too much time waiting, I often apply a wash to the page, and then work on a different part of the page while the first wash dries. Holding the page in sunlight or in the breeze can help washes dry more quickly. In any case, be patient in letting washes dry completely if subsequent washes need to have crisp edges.

In learning how to handle watercolors, especially on location, it is easiest to begin with a reasonably complete setup sketch and then fill in the spaces—sort of a paint-by-numbers approach. This is what I recommend for people who are new to watercolor. But a good challenge is to apply washes directly, without a preliminary setup sketch. This requires you to think in terms of shapes rather than outlines. The sketch in Figure 6.26 was completed in this way. The first wash was the sky, so I had to define the outline of the tower with the edges of the blue wash. The next wash defined the area of yellow and ochre that represents the building walls. Once this wash was completely dry, I added the large area of shadow on the right, and the shading on the ground. The central portal, the arches on the left, the window openings, and the roof eaves were the last elements to be added.

Figure 6.26   Watercolor without the benefit of a setup sketch. All the washes were applied as shapes to define the various elements of the view, with no initial guidelines in graphite or ink.
Santi Quattro Coronati
Rome, IT
July 10, 2011
Watercolor in Moleskine Large Watercolor Sketchbook
(5" × 8")
20 minutes

The fundamental techniques described in this chapter will allow you to achieve a wide variety of results in watercolor, and yet this medium is notoriously difficult to fully control. Sometimes you will try to apply a particular type of wash and the result will not be what you intended. These instances might feel like mistakes at first, but they often become insignificant in the context of the sketch as a whole. Try to enjoy the happy accidents of this medium, and don't be discouraged if it doesn't always behave the way you'd like. At the time when I was working on the sketch in Figure 6.27, I remember feeling frustrated by several of these "mistakes"—the fanning in the sky, for example, and the muddiness of the building on the right. Even my attempts at painting the cars just didn't seem to be working out the way I intended. But I also remember not giving up on the drawing, and looking at it now, I'm reminded that the occasionally unpredictable nature of watercolor can sometimes lead to unintentional successes.

Figure 6.27   The happy accidents of watercolor—what we perceive to be mistakes in the process of painting usually turn out to be insignificant when the sketch is complete.
Piazza Margana
Rome, IT
July 7, 2008
Watercolor on Arches Cold Press (9" × 12")
40 minutes

CHAPTER

7   *ENTOURAGE*

"Entourage" is an expression that architectural renderers have used for many years to describe the additional elements of a drawing beyond the architecture itself. These elements are typically people, landscape components, vehicles, street furniture, etc. Entourage is another word for "context," or the environment that surrounds and integrates with the aspect of the drawing most important to the sketcher. So what is considered "entourage" depends on what happens to be the primary focus of the sketch. If one's primary interest is in sketching landscapes, then perhaps architecture would be considered entourage. If one's interest is in sketching people on the street, then entourage will consist of park benches, café furniture, and the like. While entourage may be of secondary importance to the sketcher, it should not be thought of as being extraneous or unnecessary. Whatever the focus of a sketch, its context is essential. For example, if the focus is a group of people, there is a significant difference between showing those people standing on a beach, or gathered in the lobby of an opera house, or riding public transportation. If some amount of their surroundings is not part of the sketch, then it will not appear to matter where they are or what they are doing. The same is true of buildings and public spaces. If there is no suggestion of the context or the activities associated with urban places, then the sketch will misrepresent the view. If there are no people, vehicles, or street furniture shown in a public plaza, the resulting sketch will show an uninhabited, lifeless place.

Although entourage may not be the primary focus of a sketch, this should not lead to a careless approach or lack of attention toward skill development. Drawing entourage well requires as much focused practice as any other subject. In fact, entourage typically requires more practice for a simple reason—the elements of sketching that are of less interest to the artist will almost certainly receive less attention in terms of ongoing practice. While your skills for drawing architecture might be improving (if you happen to find this especially interesting to sketch), your skills for drawing other elements might not develop as quickly or as thoroughly. This can lead to sketches where there is an imbalance between the primary subject matter and the entourage—with the former being drawn quite well and the latter diminishing the quality of the sketch.

Figure 7.1 Though the primary focus of this sketch is the tower in the distance, the context (or "entourage") of the tree-lined street, the vehicles, and a few people, is critical to describing the view.
NW Johnson Street
Portland, OR
July 31, 2010
2B Pencil on Canson Classic Cream paper (9" × 12")
20 minutes

Figure 7.2   In this sketch, the building was of interest, but the activity and the crowd of people make the scene come alive
Hamilton-Lowe Aquatic Center
Moscow, ID
September 12, 2009
Copic Multiliner SP (Cobalt) in a Moleskine Pocket Sketchbook (7" × 5.5")
25 minutes

To build skills for sketching entourage, it helps to sketch these elements as much as possible as their own subject matter. For example, I regularly attend figure drawing sessions, and occasionally sketch people in public places without sketching much of their surroundings, if only for practice. I also draw or paint landscapes without any architecture or people in the view. These may not be my primary interests as a sketcher, but it is important that I build and maintain my skills in various directions, so that these elements will add to other sketches in a convincing way.

As was mentioned in Chapter 3 (in the section titled "Planning and Beginning the Sketch"), entourage must be part of the plan for a sketch from the very beginning, because these elements cannot simply be added at the end. They must to be integrated into the original setup drawing. Entourage, because it is not the primary focus, should usually be indicated in a simplified manner rather than drawn in great detail, so as not to detract from the main interest of the sketch. For example, it is sometimes sufficient to indicate groups of people or cars with a simple outline (see Figure 3.11). Try to strike a balance between accuracy, which sometimes requires detail, and indication, which often requires some level of abstraction. Abstraction requires you to know what can be left out, while still capturing the essence of what you are drawing. It may seem to be a paradox, but in order to know what can be omitted, you must practice sketching things accurately. Over time, it will become more clear how to sketch just enough of the entourage without going overboard.

People

Human figures can be one of the most difficult subjects to sketch. The complexity of faces and hands, especially, can seem too overwhelming to capture quickly and effectively on the page. While we all have great familiarity with the way people look and move, this can actually prevent us from simply sketching what we see. We carry so much visual information in our memory about all the people we have encountered that it becomes a challenge to avoid drawing what we *think* people look like, instead of carefully observing and recording what we actually see. However, when a sketch is not primarily focused on people—when it is a sketch about architecture, landscape, or public space—then they should be indicated with some abstraction rather than drawn in a detailed manner. To this end, it often helps to draw people at a distance, rather than in the foreground. The figures are there mainly to provide a sense of scale—that is, the size of the place you're sketching, and the relative sizes of people in relation to buildings, landscape elements, and public space. But in the effort of learning to trust your eyes, it can help to zero in on details, if only as a means of practice. This can prevent the problems associated with taking on too much information in a single sketch, while still learning about the way the human body appears. The sketch in Figure 7.3, for example, is my own

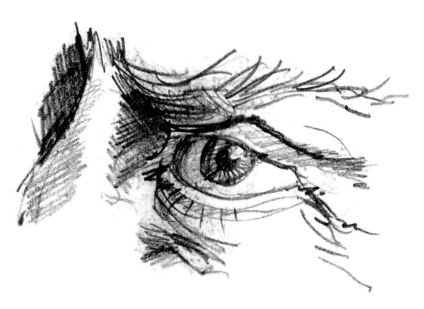

Figure 7.3   Detail sketch of an eye. Small studies such as this can be effective practice for observing and sketching human figures. 4B Pencil in Strathmore 400 Series Sketchbook (4" × 3").

Figure 7.4   Portrait studies completed during a figure-drawing session. The sketch on the left was a 5-minute pose, and the one on the right was a 10-minute one. Derwent Venetian Red Pencil on Canson Classic Cream paper (12" × 9").

eye, sketched while looking in a mirror. Taking just this small subject, rather than the entire face (or more), allowed for careful study and a greater focus on the required pencil technique. Hands and feet also make good detail subjects for practice.

Portrait drawing extends the logic of sketching individual details and further trains the eye. Someone's "likeness" is based on the relative proportions of ears, eyes, nose, mouth, and overall head structure. So if your sketch doesn't actually look like your subject, you should keep practicing until you are able to draw someone's face with accuracy. When you are able to capture a person's facial likeness, it will be evidence that you are truly using your eyes to see your subject. Closely related to portrait study is figure drawing. This is excellent practice, not only for learning how to trust your eyes and draw what you see, but also for developing an understanding of the overall human form—shapes, proportions, and relationships among the various parts of the body. In many art programs, the goal of figure drawing seems to be about free expression rather than more disciplined accuracy. No matter the approach, however, figure drawing is extremely beneficial to artists. It can be frustrating at first, but with practice figure drawing leads to greater concentration, improved technique, and enhanced ability to see and represent subtle changes in light and shade.

Figure 7.5 Three figure drawings. The two sketches on the left were approximately 3- or 4-minute poses, the one on the right was a 5-minute pose. Derwent Venetian Red Pencil on Canson Classic Cream paper (12" × 9").

One possible drawback of figure drawing is that the context is so often minimal or uninteresting. The model is usually on a small stage or platform, perhaps with a chair or other prop, and the surrounding environment is utilitarian at best. Also, in learning to draw people as entourage, it's obviously more useful to practice drawing figures that are clothed rather than nude. Coffee shops are a good place to sketch people, as the customers tend to relax and linger, and the surrounding environment is usually worth sketching. Trains and airplanes can be worthwhile places to practice sketching people at reasonably close range. I find it much easier to sketch people when they are facing away from me, as I am less distracted by the detail of their faces and I can focus on their general shape and posture.

Just be sure that you do not disturb your "subjects" by staring too intently or too long. If someone asks to see what you have been doing, it's always good etiquette to show your sketchbook. Most people will be understanding, especially if they see that your sketchbook contains many different subjects and is clearly intended for sketching practice rather than anything inappropriate. And if anyone makes it clear that they'd rather not be your sketching subject, then by all means you should apologize and stop immediately.

Figure 7.6   Sketching on airplanes, trains, or buses is good practice for drawing people at close range. Copic Multiliner SP (Wine) in a Moleskine Pocket Sketchbook (7" × 5.5").

Figure 7.7   Bars, coffee shops, and restaurants are also good places to sketch people, and the surrounding environment is usually worthwhile, too. Copic Multiliner SP (Sepia) in a Moleskine Pocket Sketchbook (7" × 5.5").

Figure 7.8 Individual figures in various poses—these are very brief drawings, perhaps just 30 seconds or so, of students in sketching class. Quick sketches of people can help with the ability to capture the overall posture and clothing without getting bogged down in detail.

To build skills for sketching people as entourage, practice making small, slightly abstracted figures on a regular basis. They may be a bit cartoonish, but this approach can be very effective when the sketch requires human figures that will not dominate the image. Practice drawing people like this in a variety of simplified poses and types of clothes, if only to prevent yourself from becoming too mechanical (i.e., sketching figures exactly the same way in all cases, like a rubber stamp). This is a common approach in the field of animation—the ability to capture posture and dress quickly and with expressive variety. If you are sketching on a bright and sunny day, it helps to indicate the direction of the light by drawing shadows cast by people. From even a small distance, these shadows will most often appear as a relatively thin and flat line of darkness starting at the feet and moving away from the position of the sun.

Figure 7.9 Small, somewhat abstracted figures can be effective, especially when gathered together in groups.

When sketching people as a way to show scale, that is, when the people are not the primary focus of the sketch, it is often most effective, and much easier, to sketch groups of figures rather than individuals. Groups of people give a better sense that a place is populated and active. I usually begin by sketching the heads and shoulders of several people, then bring the torsos and legs to the ground. Some variation of value (some figures darker and others lighter) can make the sketch quite convincing as a group of people at a slight distance (see Figure 7.9, group at lower right).

The same principles of perspective apply to people as to all other elements of sketching—the further away they are, the smaller they will appear, and the less detail will be required in their rendering. One of the rules of perspective can be very helpful to keep in mind when sketching people in public places, especially in large urban spaces. If the people within the view are all on a flat surface, their heads will appear to line up along the horizon line (provided the observer is on the same flat surface). It's easy to indicate people's distance from the viewer in this situation. Start by sketching heads at the horizon line—they will be larger if they are closer and smaller if they are farther away. Then, sketch the rest of the figures—taller if they are closer and shorter if they are in the distance (see Figure 7.10). Just remember that this phenomenon does not happen if the ground or floor is sloped rather than flat, or if the observer is viewing people from above or below.

Finally, as with all entourage elements, consider the background when deciding whether to make the figures generally light or dark in tone. If the background will be light, try to make the figures contrast with it by drawing them darker—but do pay attention to sunlight and shade, perhaps by making one side of the figure darker than the side facing the sun. If the value of the background will be dark, remember to reserve the white of the page for figures in the foreground.

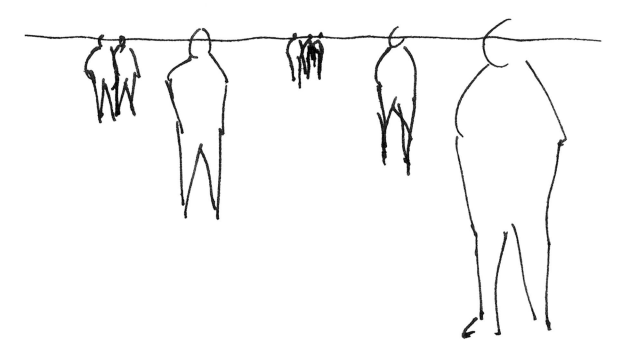

Figure 7.10   When everyone is on a flat surface, such as in a large public space, people's heads will appear to align along the horizon line.

Landscape Elements

As with people, sketching landscape elements can be intimidating. It's not uncommon for beginninners to draw trees and bushes as a spasm of squiggly lines, resulting in a sloppy, unfocused area on the page with little resemblance to foliage. It can feel as though there is too much information to take in—too many leaves, too many branches—which leads to an understandable impulse to simply cover the area on the page with a random pattern of graphite or ink. But with patience and practice—and careful observation—landscape elements can be sketched in a convincing manner, adding significantly to the overall composition of a sketch. Trust your eyes and observe, for example, how the branches of many trees reach outward and upward towards the sunlight. Begin with simple sketches of portions of trees and plants, rather than trying to tackle a giant elm or oak tree in a single sitting.

Figure 7.11 Landscape elements can provide a sense of scale, light, and spatial depth to sketches.
Temple of Poseidon
Paestum, IT
June 10, 2011
Derwent Chocolate Pencil on Canson Classic Cream Paper (12" × 9")
30 minutes

It often helps to indicate groups of foliage patterns rather than individual leaves or branches, and to strive for contrasting values to represent light and shade. Practice numerous techniques for building patterns—varying directions, small groups of hatch patterns, slightly tighter and looser groups of lines and small curves, etc. Eventually these techniques will become more comfortable and easier to execute on the page. Combing a variety of patterns and values will lead to a very effective means of representing any number of plant types and sizes.

Figure 7.12   Basic patterns useful for rendering landscape elements such as trees and shrubs. The squiggly, unfocused pattern at left is to be avoided in favor of tighter, more controlled patterns that allow you to build contrasting values.

Figure 7.13   Basic tree forms, coniferous (left) and deciduous (right).

As with sketching people, it can also help to begin by practicing small trees individually. Draw simple, free-standing trees over and over until you develop a quick technique for capturing their general form. Coniferous trees are typically very upright and focused around the central line of the trunk, and are generally pyramidal in shape—quite narrow and pointed at the top and widening toward the bottom. The upper foliage tends to reach toward the sky and the lower branches reach outward more horizontally. Varying the density of the pen or pencil strokes will give a sense of light and depth. Begin drawing deciduous trees without foliage in order to master their essential form. Notice how the limbs and branches diminish in size as they grow upward and outward, radiating from the crown of the trunk. With enough practice, these basic tree forms may be varied to represent different species and sizes of trees.

Figure 7.14 Basic value contrasts, with light foreground elements against a dark background and vice versa.

In sketching landscape elements, it is important to avoid a monotonous treatment of the subject. Even if trees and the like are drawn accurately in terms of shape and structure, they should never be drawn with a completely uniform tonal value. Changes in light and shade, whether they are subtle or dramatic, are required to indicate depth—showing that some trees and plants are nearer to the viewer than others. As discussed in Chapter 5, it often helps to shift the value of an object from light to dark, and back again, depending on the relative value of the background. Figure 7.14 is a very simple example, with the value of the tree trunk changing in relation to the vegetation beyond. This technique can be applied in many situations to emphasize the three-dimensional separation of landscape elements according to their varying distance from the observer.

Figure 7.15   Careful development of contrast, and the direction and character of pencil strokes, are essential for the accurate representation of plant material.
Biodome
Montreal, CN
March 5, 2011
2B Pencil on Aquabee Paper (9" × 12")
20 minutes

Figure 7.16   With pen, it takes more time to build up the various patterns required to represent tree trunks and foliage.
Green Lake, WI
August 1, 2011
Copic Multiliner SP (Olive) in Moleskine Large Watercolor Sketchbook (5" × 8")
30 minutes

Graphite is perhaps the easiest medium to use when sketching landscape entourage. The ability to create soft patterns of middle and light tones, and relatively hard-edged patterns of dark tones, make graphite an ideal medium for rendering landscape, particularly in the early stages of practice. Sketching landscape with pen and ink usually requires more patience in building pattern and tone. When using watercolor, the same principles apply. Focus on varying the patterns, values, and relative scales of the trees and bushes. Try to represent the way the sun lights the upper portions of trees, creates significant darkness beneath the canopies, and casts flat shadows on the ground below. Use a variety of colors to avoid applying a stereotypical "green" to all the foliage—blues, yellows, and even reds should be combined to create a vibrant representation of the plants in view.

Figure 7.17   A landscape study in watercolor.
University of Idaho Arboretum
Moscow, ID
September 30, 2011
Watercolor on Aquabee Paper (16" × 12")
60 minutes

Vehicles

As with people and landscape elements, begin your practice by drawing individual vehicles. Observe and learn to draw their general shapes and the ways that light and shade help to describe their forms. Though the lines of most contemporary cars are curved, their general volumes still tend to be somewhat boxy, and they are subject to the rules of perspective. Start by sketching overall shapes in relatively straight lines, using vanishing points as necessary to develop the general volumes with respect to the horizon line. Most automobiles are slightly shorter than the average human, so their roof line will most often be at or just below the horizon line, while the roof of a larger vehicle will be above the horizon line. Pay attention to the way cars parked along a street will sometimes slope toward the curb. As with other entourage elements, if vehicles are not the primary subject of a sketch, the details should be minimized. In most sketching situations, vehicles are seen in groups—parked along a street, for example—which can make them considerably easier to draw because only some parts of each car may be visible, such as the curve of the roof, one side of the vehicle, and one or two of the tires.

Figure 7.18   A few basic automobile sketches.

Most often, automobile interiors are in shade, so the windows can be given a dark value in contrast to the rest of the vehicle. The areas around the wheels and the ground beneath the car are also best handled with a dark shadow. You might choose to apply slightly more detail to the cars in the foreground, but it's usually best to avoid this in favor of sketching the general form and clear contrast. It's often unnecessary to show the entire vehicle in the foreground (Figure 7.1)—in fact, it may be preferable to omit most of it, so as not to distract from the primary focus of the sketch.

Figure 7.19 Cars as entourage, in the typical case where only the roofs and one side are visible.
Via di Monserrato
Rome, IT
June 11, 2008
HB Pencil on Canson Classic Cream Paper (6" × 9")
30 minutes

Street Furniture

Street furniture—park benches, tables and chairs, street signs and traffic signals, etc.—can be helpful in describing the context of a sketch. These elements, like people and vehicles, give a clear sense of scale and help to indicate the way a public space is used. However, investing too much detail in drawing street furniture, or making these elements too prominent, can significantly detract from the overall focus of a sketch. Unless the benches, signs, power lines, etc., in view contribute to the spatial character of my subject, I tend to leave most of this information out. As with all entourage elements, if the sketch is focused on street furniture, then get involved in the detail as much as you like. But if it is there for scale or context, only draw as much as is necessary to get the point across.

Figure 7.20   A pair of canvas umbrellas gives a focal element to this sketch. The light-and-shade characteristics are carefully considered, especially with regard to the background and the people standing or sitting below.
Piazza Costaguti
Rome, IT
May 30, 2007
B Pencil on Aquabee Paper (9" × 12")
20 minutes

When the street furniture is more prominent, there is an opportunity to incorporate it into the sketch more directly, especially to describe light and depth of space. The large canvas umbrellas used to shade outdoor restaurant seating are a perfect example, and they've often played a role in the sketches I have done in Italy. They are large enough to significantly contribute to the spatial character of sidewalks and public plazas, and their form is most often very clearly defined by bright sunlight above and dark shade below. Umbrellas cast dark shadows on people sitting beneath them, making it possible to sketch only their silhouettes, which is an easy way to add figures to a scene. Just remember to consider the background, and the juxtaposition of light and dark, or the street furniture in your sketch may become lost.

Figure 7.21   The grouped canvas umbrellas in market squares can help describe the scale of an urban space and a dramatic sense of light and shade.
Campo dei Fiori
Rome, IT
June 11, 2008
2B Pencil on Canson Classic Cream Paper (8" × 7")
30 minutes

Skies

In sketching with pen or pencil, I most often refrain from drawing the sky. If the subject would benefit from a dark background, to pull the buildings forward, I might include some value to indicate the sky. But in the vast majority of cases I leave it out, perhaps for fear of distracting from the focus of the sketch, which is almost always buildings, plazas, landscapes, people, etc. With watercolor, on the other hand, it is relatively easy and beneficial to include a simple blue wash to indicate a light-filled and transparent sky. A wet-into-wet technique works well, starting with clean water on the page and introducing Cerulean or Ultramarine, or a mix of both. By letting the wash migrate on the page, interesting effects can be achieved without much effort. In any case, I try to avoid an over-worked sky with billowing clouds. But this may just be my personal preference. If skies are interesting to you, experiment with and practice various techniques in different media. In watercolor, using a simple wet-into-wet technique can create swirling cloud effects. First wet the page, then introduce Cerulean and/ or Ultramarine Blue. Let the pigment migrate before soaking up excess water with the brush or paper towel.

Figure 7.22 A simple sky in watercolor, using a wet-into-wet technique with Cerulean Blue.
San Silvestro in Capite
Rome, IT
July 2, 2010
Watercolor in Moleskine Large Watercolor Sketchbook (5" × 8")
40 minutes

Figure 7.23   On a cloudy, rainy day, the sky will be relatively dark and more of a gray/purple rather than light blue.
Villa Giulia
Rome, IT
May 28, 2010
Uniball Vision Micro and Watercolor in Moleskine Large Watercolor Sketchbook (8" × 5")
30 minutes

Carefully observe the colors of clouds and their shading characteristics. They tend to be very light above, either pure white or a warm off-white, and darker below, in shades of gray and purple. During the day, when the sun is high, the color of the sky is typically a clear Cerulean Blue. In the early morning, and especially in the evening, the color of the sky can be extremely variable. There are usually shades of rich blue (Cerulean, Prussian, and/or Ultramarine), but there are often numerous other colors—yellow, gold, peach, salmon, violet, or even green. In monochromatic sketches, simply focus on relative values—is the sky dark behind light clouds, or vice versa? Can the sky or clouds be used to contrast with other aspects of the sketch? A deep, dark, night sky, for example, may be used to contrast dramatically with lighted buildings. But if the buildings, trees, or other sketched elements need to be darker, then the best strategy for the sky might be to leave it alone, and let the white of the page serve as the contrast to shaded elements in the near distance.

Figure 7.24   View from San Pietro in Montorio
Rome, IT
June 23, 2009
Watercolor on Arches Cold Press (12" × 9")
45 minutes

CHAPTER

8 *AFTER SKETCHING*

Figure 8.1 Delta Flight #130
March 18, 2010
Copic Multiliner SP (Olive) and Watercolor in Hand-Book Journal (10" × 8")
35 minutes

As you sketch more frequently, you will likely accumulate numerous sketchbooks and portfolios full of your work. Storing and protecting the physical drawings, and cataloguing the digital image files, will require you to develop some simple techniques, strategies, and habits. For some, sketching will be a purely personal endeavor, and for others, sharing their work will become more important. Regardless of your personal inclination, I encourage you to find ways to share your work as a way to build skills and make connections with other sketchers. If your sketches will be printed or shared online, then it helps to learn processes for making good digital or photographic reproductions. And finally, there are many venues through which your sketches might be displayed, from local galleries to online forums. Presented here are my suggestions for storing, reproducing, and sharing your sketches, and ideas for making connections with other sketchers.

Storing and Protecting Sketches

Sketches are most commonly drawn in sketchbooks, and it might be assumed that they would be sufficiently protected that way. But this depends on the type of sketchbook, the type of media used for the sketches, and the way the sketchbook is treated by its owner. Hardcover sketchbooks, especially those equipped with an elastic band, tend to do the best job of protecting the drawings inside. Ring-bound sketchbooks, for all their other advantages, do not offer as much protection as hardcover books. Their covers tend to slip in opposing directions, making the pages rub against one another inside the closed book. If you have used graphite, charcoal, or other dry media, your sketches may become smudged. One remedy for this is to wrap a large rubber band around the cover, or use large binder clips to hold the cover tightly in place when you are not sketching. Sketches that are drawn on loose sheets of paper are best carried and stored in a portfolio with clear plastic sleeves. Itoya is a brand that makes portfolios in a variety of sizes, such as 8½" × 11" and 9" × 12", and they are of good quality. In any case, it makes sense to store all of your books and portfolios in one place for easy reference and organization.

Figure 8.2 My personal collection of sketchbooks, as of November 2010. Some are full of drawings, and others are waiting to be used for the first time. Some are not actually sketchbooks but portfolios full of loose-leaf sketches that have been removed from ring-bound pads of paper or watercolor blocks.

Figure 8.3   Tracing paper taped to a sketchbook page in order to protect dry media from smudging.

When working with dry media, such as graphite or charcoal, it may be tempting to apply spray fixatives to prevent smudging. While there may be types or brands of fixative that will not damage your sketches over time, I would not take the chance. I once used spray fixative on several graphite sketches that I drew as a student in Rome. The damage did not appear until about three to five years later, but then the paper began to turn splotchy and yellow, and the sketches were effectively ruined. Other sketches from that time—ones not sprayed with fixative—were still in perfect condition 25 years later. After this experience, I devised a simple strategy for protecting my sketches, especially those drawn with dry media. Cut sheets of tracing paper to size and tape them directly to the page with drafting tape. If the sketchbook pages rub together, the tracing paper moves with the page and prevents the facing page from smearing the sketch. Tracing paper is very thin and lightweight, so it will not add bulk to your sketchbook. It is also reasonably transparent, so the sketch can be seen through the paper, but I usually just tape two corners down, so that the paper can be lifted up to see the sketch without having to remove the tracing paper entirely. Drafting tape is preferable to masking or transparent tape, because its adhesive is not so strong, and it will not likely damage the sketchbook paper if it is removed.

Reproducing Sketches

In order to print or share your sketches in a digital format, they first need to be either scanned or photographed. Scanning is the most common method of digitizing sketches, though photography can yield superior results if it is done properly. The general goal, regardless of technique, should be to capture a faithful image—the reproduction should look as much like the sketch as possible. Whether you photograph or scan, take the time to learn the best process, and take notes so that you don't need to relearn the most effective techniques each time you have a group of drawings to reproduce.

Scanning sketches can be a time-consuming process, so it's a good idea to get the best possible scan the first time. You want to avoid having to re-scan sketches because it was done poorly the first time, or because you need a higher-resolution image at a later date. Develop a work-flow that effectively captures your drawings and be consistent—this makes the scanning process smooth, and saves time whenever you have new sketches to scan. Use the best scanner you can find, as inexpensive scanners might not capture subtle color variation. Be sure that the scanner's glass plate (known as the *platen*) is clean and dust-free, or you may end up with unwanted marks on the digital image. Press the page down evenly as the scan is being made. Watercolor paper, especially, has a tendency to buckle and not lay flat against the glass, which can create uneven lighting and focus. Scan at high resolution, at least 300 dpi. Ink sketches scan quite well at medium resolution, but low- or medium-resolution scans of graphite and watercolors can be especially problematic. Graphite tends to become severely pixelated, and faint watercolor may not show up at all—especially the very light blues. The higher the resolution of the scan, the more likely these problems will not crop up. Scanner drivers (the software interface between the computer and the scanner) allow for many adjustments to the image in the act of making the scan, such as brightness, contrast, and color balance. I recommend setting all of these adjustments to neutral positions in order to get the truest image possible. If adjustments are made with the scanner driver, then the resulting image will be unfaithful to the original, and this is not a good place to begin. Corrections can be made after scanning by using image editing software, such as Adobe Photoshop, but only if you have captured an accurate image first.

An alternative to scanning is to photograph your sketches. This may be done professionally, which is the surest way to get an accurate reproduction of the sketch. Professional photography studios will have high-quality lighting and camera equipment, and a technician with a good eye will be able to handle any necessary color-correction issues. If the quality of the reproduction is your top priority, this is the best approach, though the service does come at a price. Expect to pay $50 or so per image, which will usually include at least one printed proof and color correction.

Figure 8.4   A professionally photographed sketch. Even the very light blues of the sky are captured faithfully, which can be a problem with scanning.
Temple of Aesculapius
Rome, IT
June 13, 2008
Watercolor on Arches Cold Press (12" × 9")
30 minutes

Figure 8.5 Photographing sketches in full sunlight can be a quick alternative to scanning or an affordable alternative to professional photography.
Largo do Chiado
Lisbon, PT
July 21, 2011
Watercolor in Moleskine Large Watercolor Sketchbook (5" × 16")
45 minutes

If the cost of professional photography seems prohibitive, or if you simply prefer to do it yourself, excellent results can be had with a reasonably good digital camera. Lighting is the most important factor in doing your own photography. It is best to use professional-quality lighting—desk lamps will not work—but in a pinch, you can rely on the sun. I took the photo in Figure 8.5 immediately after completing the sketch, so I would be ready to upload the image the next time I had access to a computer. A well-focused, sunlit digital photo can be one of the best reproduction options. Some simple cropping and perhaps a bit of lens correction can produce an excellent digital image of the sketch. Try to take photos in full, direct sunlight, as close to mid-day as possible. Place the paper or sketchbook on a surface with a neutral color—nonreflective black cloth is the best backdrop, but a sheet of white paper can work. Even the sidewalk or pavement will do, as long as it is a neutral color—beige or gray are usually fine. Position the image so that the sun is shining directly on it rather than at an angle, and hold the camera perpendicular to the page, about three or four feet away. Zoom in to eliminate as much of the surrounding ground as possible. It sometimes takes a little maneuvering to get in the correct position without casting a shadow on the page. Be sure to align the drawing as well as possible in the camera's viewfinder, so that the image is not skewed in any direction, as this makes cropping easier. Once you are ready, take a few pictures. Experiment with bracketing and white balance until you get the desired results. Focus is important—you want the image to be perfectly sharp. A tripod can be helpful, but is not usually necessary to get a clear and focused image in very bright sunlight. If your hands are not steady, however, a tripod might be required to achieve the best focus. If the photograph is clear and well lit, editing in Photoshop or a similar program will be minimal.

Sharing Sketches and Sketching with Others

The simplest and most direct way to share your drawings is to open your sketchbook to those around you. Too often, we assume that others are not interested or that our sketches are not "good enough" to be displayed or discussed. But this is never the case. Regardless of how we perceive the quality of our own work, sketching is an inherently interesting activity that generates communication on many levels. The drawings may be discussed on their own merits, but most often they act as catalysts for social interaction. They encourage us to communicate about the subject matter, the media, the experiences of places we've been, people we have met, or food we have enjoyed. The more we share our work and generate these connections with others, the more we see the deeper values of sketching on location.

Figure 8.6   An exhibit of sketches at a local gallery.

Another way of sharing your work is to seek out opportunities for exhibition. Small galleries often wish to display the work of local artists, and coffee shops and restaurants are also potential venues. Whether you're actively trying to sell your drawings, or you're only interested in displaying them to a larger audience, local exhibitions are a good place to begin. You will likely develop some connections with other local artists, which might lead to group exhibits or other opportunities. If you plan to display original work in a public space, be sure to consider security, especially if you will be showing a sketchbook. You don't want random people to be able to flip through your sketchbook because they can leave fingerprints or otherwise damage the sketches or the binding. Placing an open book under a glass frame can work. An alternative is to reproduce the work as discussed above, and display prints rather than originals. This is a compromise, as it is almost always more interesting to see originals, but for the safety of your work, this might be the most favorable option.

Forum
um, IT
ne II, 2010
Watercolor on Arches Cold Press
(9" × 12")
45 minutes

Because sketch artists live all over the world, viewing their work online provides an opportunity to travel vicariously through their drawings—and an opportunity for others to visit the places where you live and travel. The venues for sharing location sketches online are many and varied, but they generally fall into a few categories—weblogs, photo-sharing sites, and forums. Most blogs are created by individual artists, where they can periodically post a few sketches and write a about the experience they had while drawing, or a description of the subject or the media. Some blogs are more elaborate than others and some bloggers post daily entries while others post less frequently. There are also group blogs, oriented around particular cities or subjects, such as "Sketching in Nature," which, as the blog title would suggest, is a group of artists whose subject matter consists mainly of landscapes, flora and fauna. One of the more prominent group blogs devoted to location drawing is "Urban Sketchers," a group of about one hundred "correspondents" (myself included), created by a Seattle resident, Gabriel Campanario. We are called correspondents because one of the goals of the blog is to create graphic and textual reportage from our respective cities. Through my involvement in Urban Sketchers, I have met and sketched on location with many people on my travels with whom I would never have connected otherwise.

Figure 8.8 Piazza del Duomo
Spoleto, IT
June 20, 2008
B Pencil on Canson Drawing Paper (12" × 9")
40 minutes

Photo-sharing sites are also an important aspect of online social networking among sketchers, with Flickr being the most commonly used site for this purpose. These sites are primarily used by people sharing photographs, but there are a growing number of sketch artists using the site exclusively for their artwork. Each participant is able to post as many sketches as they like, organizing them with subject- or media-oriented tags, and grouping them into sets. Each sketch can be place-marked on a map, showing where it was made. Groups are created within Flickr to bring together images in a particular vein—"Location Drawing" is one example, "Urban Sketchers" is another—and by submitting sketches to these groups, an artist can effectively publish their work to an interested and receptive audience. The site allows members to collect "favorite" images from other artists, and it keeps track of who has identified your work as a favorite. Each image may be commented upon, which often creates a lively conversation among the participants.

Figure 8.9   San Clemente
Rome, IT
July 10, 2011
Watercolor on Arches Cold Press
(9" × 12")
60 minutes

Forums are dedicated websites that allow threaded discussions under a general heading. Most forums require registration as a member in order to contribute new subject threads or to comment on existing threads, but are otherwise open to anyone for viewing. "The Sketching Forum" is an example of a well-established site, with a "Sketch Talk" section including a variety of topics and a "Sketch Gallery" section where participants show their work. The tone of this forum is uniformly inquisitive and supportive, with a wide array of topics, often focused on media and technique. Another example is the "SketchCrawl Forum." In 2002, Enrico Casarosa, a storyboard artist with Pixar Animation Studios, created the first SketchCrawl—a term derived from "PubCrawl," and expressive of a similar social dynamic. In Casarosa's words, SketchCrawls are about "having people from different corners of the world join in a day of sketching and journaling and then, thanks to the Internet, having everyone share the results on an online forum." Worldwide sketchcrawls now take place four or five times each year, involving hundreds of contributors from cities around the world. These events have also spawned regular meetings of sketchers on the local level—in cites large and small there are often groups that gather informally to sketch together and share their work. It is through these opportunities that individuals can connect with others, build their skills, and be exposed to other approaches and media choices.

Figure 8.10   La Spiaggia
Atrani, IT
June 7, 2008
HB Pencil on Canson Drawing Paper (12" × 9")
40 minutes

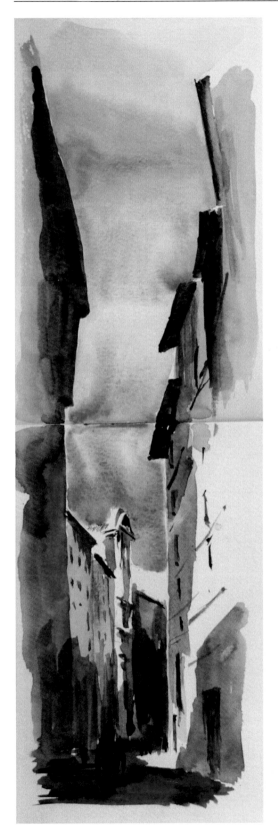

Online and local networking associated with location drawing is not limited to blogs, photo-sharing sites, forums, and sketchcrawls. "SketchTravel" is a site that facilitates the sharing of a single, physical sketchbook among participants around the world. The book is mailed from person to person, with each artist typically filling one spread with drawing. In this case, the subject matter is not exclusively location drawing, but it represents another way of using the Internet to make connections among artists with a similar ethic for sharing their work. It is this ethic of interaction and exchange that is the hallmark of online networking where it meets with location drawing. Throughout these interactions, there is a clear focus on exposure to a variety of media and technique, subject matter, and cultures—with personal connections developing around the passion and craft of sketching on location.

Figure 8.11   Via di Monserrato
Rome, IT
July 16, 2011
Watercolor in Moleskine Large Watercolor Sketchbook (5" × 16")
35 minutes

Final Thoughts

I first began to sketch as part of an architectural degree program, but, in the years since, I have made sketching my own. It is an integral aspect of my life and of the way I relate to the world around me. Sketching is not a "pastime" or a trivial hobby. It is instead a tremendously productive and edifying activity. Sketching is a craft, bringing with it a sense of pride and accomplishment in creating something of lasting value by hand. Sketching is a visual record of my life, the places where I have lived and traveled. Sketching is a way to make new acquaintances—by sharing my work through numerous venues over the years, I've had the good fortune to meet and sketch with many wonderful people. When I sketch, I am part of an extremely long artistic tradition, one that goes back thousands of years. This tradition will surely continue to flourish, as communicating through drawing is one of the fundamental characteristics that makes us human.

Perhaps more than any other reason, I sketch because I've found it to be a powerful way to learn about the world. When I observe and try to sketch a building or a place, I engage in a process of discovery and understanding. Although most location sketches take only 20 or 30 minutes to complete, this time adds up quickly, and it is quality time spent actually studying and being engaged with my environment, rather than rushing through with my eyes glued to the screen of a telephone. After sketching, I have a visual record of what I've learned, and a

Figure 8.12   Prichard Gallery
Moscow, ID
March 17, 2009
Copic Multiliner (Olive) in Moleskine Pocket Sketchbook (7" × 5.5")
20 minutes

Figure 8.13   Santa Maria in Trastevere
Rome, IT
July 2, 2008
HB Pencil on Canson Drawing Paper (9" × 12")
55 minutes

touchstone to my experience of a place, so the learning can continue every time I refer to a particular drawing or sketchbook. Taken as a whole, I've not found a better way to learn about the world than by sketching on location.

Sometimes, depending on the subject or situation, sketching can be exciting and challenging. But in most cases there is no pressure, no set of expectations looming over your head. Sketching is simple and relaxing. It encourages me to slow down and pay attention. In this regard, I would venture to say that sketching is healthy for mind and body, as it can be a form of meditation or mindfulness. It has been shown that meditation has

Figure 8.14   Lawsonia Barns
Green Lake, WI
August 3, 2011
Watercolor in Moleskine Large Watercolor Sketchbook (16" × 5")
45 minutes

numerous health benefits, from lowered blood pressure to a healthier immune system—and I would not be surprised if frequent sketching produced similar results in clinical tests. The potential health benefits, the unique type of learning, the sense of craft, the connection to an artistic tradition, the social connections—these are some of the more prominent reasons why I continue to sketch on a regular basis. And yet, even if none of these aspects of sketching were present—even if sketching were not so deeply rewarding on so many levels, I would likely still do it, just because it's fun. When all else fails, sketching is a simple pleasure that may be enjoyed by anyone with pencil and paper.

This book represents my current understandings of how to sketch on location, but I continue to learn. The more I sketch and meet others who sketch, the more I discover new techniques and worthwhile approaches to unique situations. Happily, there is always more to learn about sketching, and there is always more to learn by sketching. I sincerely hope that this book has been inspirational as well as informative. All a teacher can do is guide and encourage others, and point in a direction that he or she has found useful. This has been my goal. But to achieve personal satisfaction in an endeavor like sketching, there is no substitute for doing it frequently, thoughtfully, and with purpose. Become your own teacher. Celebrate your successes and learn from your failures, but always keep sketching. It's a big world, and sketching on location is the best way I know of to explore, learn about, understand, and enjoy it.

Figure 8.15 Forum Romanum
Rome, IT
July 9, 2011
Watercolor on Arches Cold Press (9" × 12")
40 minutes

SELECTED BIBLIOGRAPHY

Moh'd Bilbeisi. *Graphic Journaling*. Kendall Hunt Publishing Company: Dubuque, IA, 2009.

Gabriel Campanario. *The Art of Urban Sketching*. Quarry Books: Beverly, MA, 2012.

Francis D.K. Ching. *Architectural Graphics*. John Wiley & Sons: New York, 2009.

Norman Crowe & Paul Laseau. *Visual Notes for Architects and Designers*. John Wiley & Sons: New York, 1984.

Michael Doyle. *Color Drawing*. John Wiley & Sons: New York, 1999.

Donald A. Gerds. *Perspective, Seventh Edition*. DAG Design: Manhattan Beach, CA, 2006.

Danny Gregory. *An Illustrated Life*. How Books: Cincinnati, OH, 2008.

Arthur L. Guptill. *Sketching and Rendering in Pencil*. The Pencil Points Press: New York, 1922.

Erwin Herzberger. *Freehand Drawing for Architects and Designers*. Whitney Library of Design: New York, 1988.

Ron Kasprisin. *Design Media*. John Wiley & Sons: New York, 1999.

Stephen Kliment. *Architectural Sketching and Rendering*. Whitney Library of Design: New York, 1984.

Peter A. Koenig. *Design Graphics*. Prentice Hall: Upper Saddle River, NJ, 2012.

Paul Laseau. *Freehand Sketching*. W.W. Norton: New York, 1999.

Mike W. Lin. *Architectural Rendering Techniques*. John Wiley & Sons: New York, 1985.

William Kirby Lockard. *Design Drawing*. W.W. Norton: New York, 2001.

John Montague. *Basic Perspective Drawing: A Visual Approach*. John Wiley & Sons: New York, 1998.

Thomas Wang. *Pencil Sketching, Second Edition*. John Wiley & Sons: New York, 2002.

Edward T. White. *Travel Drawing: Engaging the Spirit of Place*. Architectural Media Publishers: Tallahassee, FL, 2004.

Magali Delgao Yanes. *Freehand Drawing for Architects and Interior Designers*. W.W. Norton: New York, 2004.

Online Resources

Author Blog: brehmsketch.blogspot.com

Author Flickr Page: www.flickr.com/photos/mtbrehm/

Urban Sketchers: www.urbansketchers.com

Worldwide SketchCrawl: www.sketchcrawl.com

SketchTravel: www.sketchtravel.com

The Sketching Forum: www.sketching.cc/forum3/

INDEX